'We have been very early adopters of talking therapie[...]
PSTEC and hypnotherapy –] and anecdotally believe [...]
important of all our interventions for keeping weight [...] [...]
detailed insight into these techniques and how successful they can be.'

Dr Matthew S Capehorn, Clinical Director, National Obesity Forum and
Clinical Manager, Rotherham Institute for Obesity

'I believe the work Sally and Liz are doing is the missing link between
knowing what we should be eating and actually doing so.'

Barry Groves, Researcher and author of *Natural Health and Weight Loss* and
Trick and Treat

What our clients say:

'No-one is more surprised than me. I get on the scales every week and every
week I've lost a few more pounds. I kept waiting for it to stop working –
nothing works for me – but this does, and the weight is still coming off me!'

'I had decided to go for sessions in order to lose weight. However, I got more
than that. I lost weight in the weeks I was attending the sessions, and I am
still losing now. I am on holiday right now and went off the plan. After two
days my mind and body easily switched back. I have been programmed not
to fail!'

'I don't even notice the biscuits and cakes at work now. It's not like I feel I'm
denying myself. It's hard to put my finger on it, but I don't even notice them
anymore. It feels easy; I'm just not interested in eating that kind of stuff
anymore.'

'I have a meal and I'm enjoying eating it as usual. After a while I look at the food and think to myself – you know what, I don't want any more. It feels like I'm really smiling inside because it just feels natural, and easy to leave it – nothing at all to do with will-power.'

'Working with PSTEC and EFT has changed my life! I've lost 7 kilos in eight weeks, am happier than I have been in a long time, and I am taking control of my life at last. I would recommend working this way without hesitation – it has worked for me on so many levels!'

'I feel finally able to clear away the physical and "emotional" fat to allow my true self to shine out there in the world. You have supported me to learn how to do this for myself, on my own. I can really do this!!!'

'I always knew that the reasons for my difficulty in losing weight were hidden deep inside of me. I needed to find the way in there to deal with it. This has helped release old stuff with very little pain.'

'I have made significant and positive changes to my life and there is now potential for who knows what? I do know though that I am working on it, and I feel so much more hopeful about my future.'

'Food no longer feels like an ugly demon. Instead it's something I can manage and enjoy. And, you've given me my confidence back!'

'I am a chocoholic who has not had chocolate for two months and I don't miss it!'

For more go to page 189.

Seven Simple Steps to Stop Emotional Eating

targeting your body by changing your mind

This book is dedicated to my husband, the painter Arnold Dobbs, and to my wonderful son Eliot Breen, who together have given me their unwavering support every step of the way. I love you both with all my heart.

Sally Baker

I would like to dedicate this book to my three children, who have all been amazing inspirations in my life.

Liz Hogon

Seven Simple Steps to Stop Emotional Eating

targeting your body by changing your mind

Sally Baker & Liz Hogon

Foreword by
Dr Matthew S Capehorn

Hammersmith Health Books
London, UK

First published in 2015 by Hammersmith Health Books – an imprint of
Hammersmith Books Limited
14 Greville Street, London EC1N 8SB, UK
www.hammersmithbooks.co.uk

Disclaimer: The information in this book is of a general nature and is meant for educational purposes only. It is not intended as medical advice. The contents may not be used to treat, or diagnose, any particular disease, or any particular person. Applying elements from this publication does not constitute a professional relationship, or professional advice, or services. Please consult your own medical or mental health practitioner(s), if this is appropriate, with regard to your own personal emotional or psychological issues before using any of the therapeutic self-help techniques described in this book.

The testimonials and opinions expressed by the individuals who have contributed content at the start of this book are theirs alone. No endorsement or warranty is explicit or implied by any entity connected to this content. All testimonies are guaranteed one hundred per cent genuine, and are provided to illustrate the variety of ways in which the therapies described in the book have worked for clients.

Please note: Original correspondence is available for inspection by advertising standards authorities. Some testimonials have been edited for reasons of brevity and clarity, or to protect identities. No absolute claim is made that you will receive identical levels of success.

British Library Cataloguing in Publication Data: a CIP record of this book is available from the British Library.

Print ISBN: 978-1-78161-058-9
Ebook ISBN: 978-1-78161-059-6

Editor: Georgina Bentliff
Cover and illustrations and worksheet design: Annie Rickard Straus
Text designed and typeset by: Julie Bennett of Bespoke Publishing Ltd
Index: Jan Ross of Merrall-Ross International Ltd
Production: Helen Whitehorn of Path Projects Ltd
Printed and bound by: TJ International Ltd

Contents

Acknowledgements

We would like to thank Tim Phizackerley, the creator of Percussive Suggestion Technique (PSTEC), for his tireless encouragement and support for our work. We feel privileged to know both him and his wife Karen, and count them as friends; We feel very fortunate to continue our professional relationship with the Hawaiian-based Jeff Harding, also a fellow PSTEC Master Practitioner, and our favoured go-to for our web-based presence. Annie Rickard Straus' illustrative skill and unique style has added another positive dimension to our book. She has been a joy to work with. We would also like to express our gratitude for this opportunity to our Commissioning Editor at Hammersmith Health Books, Georgina Bentliff, for seeing the potential for *Seven Simple Steps*'s in-depth approach in our earlier, embryonic e-book. Finally thanks are due to the late Barry Groves PhD, a pioneering health crusader, who also at an early stage saw the value of our therapeutic approach to resolve and release issues around emotional eating for successful weight loss.

In conclusion, we would like to thank our clients who have taught us so much. We are especially grateful to those who volunteered to be case studies for this book as well as the hundreds of others we have worked successfully with over the years. We are often humbled by the courage and determination we bear witness to in overcoming some of life's less than positive circumstances and experiences, plus the humour and grace expressed in the face of great adversity. May they all continue to thrive.

Foreword

We are currently facing an epidemic of obesity and diabetes that could bankrupt the NHS and affect the quality of life of millions of people. Over recent years there has been increasing focus on the psychological barriers to successful and sustainable weight loss, with an appreciation of the need to address the underlying causes for why we overeat and become overweight or obese.

Behaviour change has been shown to be an important part of the multi-disciplinary approach to weight loss, and is likely to be the vital factor in maintaining any weight loss. Comfort eating, habit eating and other self-sabotaging behaviours can result in unsuccessful weight-loss interventions or may be factors in why we regain any weight lost, which may in turn lead to a sense of failure and decreased motivation. It makes sense that whether we lose weight through diet and exercise, or weight-loss medications, or very low-calorie diets, or even bariatric surgery, if we do not address the underlying reasons why we became overweight in the first place we are at increased risk of putting that weight back on.

The term 'talking therapy' has become common-place to describe interventions that aim to help identify the emotional issues that underlie problems such as over- or under-eating, and teach individuals the techniques to manage them. The term is wide ranging and can be used to include holistic approaches more associated with life-coaching, for the identification of barriers and appropriate goal-setting, together with motivational interviewing. However, it also includes techniques to help facilitate the behaviour changes required. This can include established techniques such as cognitive behavioural therapy (CBT), but also neuro-linguistic programming (NLP), emotional freedom technique (EFT), percussive suggestion technique (PSTEC) and hypnotherapy, which all work in different ways, allowing therapies to be tailored to the individual. At the Rotherham Institute for Obesity we were very early adopters of talking therapies, and anecdotally believe these to be the most important of all our interventions for keeping weight off. Practitioners working within the field of weight management need to embrace talking therapies, consider their use for appropriate individuals, and help to add to the evidence base to allow us to know which interventions are most effective for tackling obesity. This book gives a detailed insight into some of these techniques, and how successful they can be.

Dr Matthew S Capehorn
Clinical Director, National Obesity Forum (NOF)
Clinical Manager, Rotherham Institute for Obesity (RIO)

About the authors

We met by chance in North London more than 15 years ago and instantly became good friends as well as growing to become enduring professional colleagues.

Although when we met we were already busy building up our own general therapy practices, we decided to work together as co-facilitators delivering a series of weekly group-therapy weight-loss workshops in London. Working in this way allowed us the chance to originate, design and create a therapeutic course of our own, based on our shared interest.

Central to our work, now as then, is the discovery and releasing of the underlying reasons for emotional eating and emotional obesity, which we continue to believe are the key to successful long-term weight loss.

We are qualified to work in this field for several reasons. First, of course, there are our many years of therapeutic training (see below), and our professional qualifications, often to trainer, or advanced level, in several modalities, including hypnotherapy, emotional freedom technique (EFT) and, in more recent years, Master Practitioner level in percussive suggestion technique (PSTEC).

We are also empathetically qualified for this work as we have both watched with dismay our own waistlines expand in our late 40s and 50s. We have both been married and divorced, and one of us (Sally) has happily married again in recent years. We have both raised children, now grown up, of whom we are very proud, and spent years keeping our homes together, mostly on our own, while often doing two jobs. We too have faced the prospect of feeling invisible in a youth-obsessed world. We have felt hot and cold in quick succession, and come out the other side, feeling able, finally and fully, to step into our own power, and it feels wonderful!

We are the sum of everything that has ever happened to us and everything we have ever done – the positive and the negative. It informs and enriches who we are, and our work. We too are works in progress.

Over the years we have continued to learn, and refine, the therapy tools we use by working one-to-one with clients to allow them to end emotional eating and achieve their weight-loss goals.

This book is a distillation of how we work with clients in our own private practices. Thank goodness for modern technology as we are now living on different sides of the globe.

We hope, and trust, that by following our *Seven Simple Steps to Stop Emotional Eating* you will be able to learn, and use for yourself, the therapy tools we have found to be most effective, so that you too can free yourself, gently and non-judgementally, from your entanglements with food to lose excess weight, and step into your power too.

All we ask is that you treat yourself always with kindness and forgiveness while you do the work. If you question and doubt your own past behaviour – if you focus on times when you wish you had behaved differently – know that you were only ever doing the best you could at that time.

Breathe, and let go.

Sally and Liz

Sally Baker

Sally Baker is a full-time therapist and writer who has been working for over a decade in private practice in London. She sees clients, both face-to-face and the world over via Skype, for a wide range of presenting issues. Her professional specialism and passion is the development and application of effective therapeutic approaches to help clients resolve and release the reasons for emotional eating so that they can achieve and maintain successful weight loss. As well as being a hypnotherapist, she is a Master Practitioner of PSTEC (percussive suggestion technique), and she is an

Advanced Practitioner of EFT (emotional freedom technique).

Born in Birmingham in 1956, Sally came to London for a weekend when she was 21, and has stayed ever since. Her first job was as a trainee journalist based in Soho, writing about television and film. After 10 years of magazine publishing and editing, she made the move from theory to practice, working in visual effects production for top-end commercials, music videos and feature films.

Sally married for the first time in 1984. The marriage ended in divorce seven years later, leaving her a single parent to their five-year-old son. She continued to work in the media while juggling the demands of raising her son with those of doing a full-time job. In 2000 she met her second husband, the painter Arnold Dobbs, who welcomed both Sally and her son into his life. Two years later he offered her an invaluable opportunity when he suggested she take a break from working to discover what she would really like to do with her life.

She turned her attention to formal study and graduated with an Advanced Certificate in Post-Compulsory Education from Canterbury University. She went on to be employed as a tutor teaching young adults with severe learning difficulties at an inner-city college for over five years.

Sally has a long-term interest in the mind-body connection and its vital role in wellbeing and mental health. Around this time she qualified in holistic (Swedish) massage and was drawn to working with women survivors of sexual and physical abuse. She soon came to realise she needed more resources to enable her to hold a safe space for their emotional distress. Liz Hogon, her friend, co-writer and fellow therapist, whom she had met in the same week as she had met her second husband, introduced her to EFT. It proved to be an effective therapeutic approach to enable her clients to release their traumatic experiences and to feel more accepting of themselves.

The therapy element of her work became her main focus. Reducing her teaching hours, she undertook more advanced therapeutic training and research until this work became her sole occupation.

The experience of working in her own private practice, and the close collaboration she enjoys with Liz, have formed the basis and inspiration for *The Seven Simple Steps to Stop Emotional Eating*.

Liz Hogon

A qualified, full-time therapist since 2001, Liz Hogon has helped thousands of people overcome issues surrounding emotional eating, smoking, phobias and chronic anxiety. She became interested in alternative therapies when she failed to recover from a severe bout of Ross River fever in her native Australia. This debilitating mosquito-borne virus attacks the immune system and left her exhausted, with no medical resolution. Of all the therapeutic approaches she explored, it was emotional freedom technique (EFT) that proved to be the most effective in increasing her energy levels and reducing her neurological symptoms.

As a therapist, Liz became frustrated for clients who were battling emotional eating and arrived with arm-long lists of interventions they had unsuccessfully tried: expensive diet programmes, traditional therapies and even surgical procedures. She also realised that hypnotherapy was often a short-term fix, and that suggestions could wear off, leaving people to revert without having resolved the psychological issues that caused the emotional eating in the first place.

Liz sought lasting solutions to these problems and was the first to use PSTEC for emotional eating. It had previously only been used for negative feelings, with which it had enjoyed enormous success. Liz, along with Sally, has developed the specialist approach recommended in this book, which successfully addresses at a very deep level the psychological factors that create emotional eating, and uses these tools daily in her successful clinic in Melbourne, Australia.

Prior to her return to Australia, Liz worked full-time in her busy private practice in London. She initially trained there in hypnotherapy before becoming an advanced therapist and trainer in EFT. More recently, she was invited to become a Master Practitioner of PSTEC (percussive suggestion technique).

Liz's children are all grown now and she moved back to Australia in 2010 to allow herself time with her growing brood of grandchildren. She settled in Melbourne where she has established a cutting-edge therapeutic practice. Liz is committed to Continuing Professional Development (CPD) and has also qualified in several other modalities.

NOTE: In writing this book, we have changed the names of our personal clients and not revealed their geographical locations in order to maintain their anonymity. It should be noted, however, that each of us has our own private practice and we do not see clients together as a team.

Introduction

What is 'emotional eating'?

> Too much on your plate?
> Swallowing down your anger with food?
> Frustrated at your yo-yo dieting?
> Eating when bored, or on your own?
> Feeling out of control around food?
> Eating in secret?
> Bingeing and purging?
> Feeling sad and eating to fill a void inside?
> Rewarding yourself with food after a hard day?

Let's first be clear, and define emotional eating as a behaviour that occurs only in the developed world, the lands of perceived plenty. Negative self-judgements; obsessive over-thinking about calories; skipping meals; bingeing and purging; or any of the other many aspects of emotional eating do not exist in countries of food scarcity or where people struggle for survival. It's noteworthy that as third world countries emerge economically onto the world stage they open their doors to western influences and their seductive power. The socially mobile classes of any indigenous population quickly develop a taste for western fashion, and music, as well as western foods. The Standard American Diet of refined carbohydrates, calorie-dense fast-foods and fizzy drinks is now exported all over the world. Adopting it is a way of aping western consumption, and values, and can be found in the cities of China, Russia and India, as well, increasingly, as in more remote outposts. It also causes sectors of the population of these countries to judge themselves negatively against the narrow, westernised standard of perfection. With that comes self-dissatisfaction – a step on the road to emotional eating that was not apparent just a few decades ago.

The pressure to be perfect

Over-thinking about food and negative self-judgements, both of which are key indicators of emotional eating, require a level of compliance to socially accepted norms. In the West the definition of an acceptable body-type for women, and increasingly for men, is force-fed to us through the media, and imposes an impossible ideal. Unattainable standards of physical perfection are loudly proclaimed on all media platforms by 'body fascists' who deride anyone, especially the famous, who fails to comply with their narrow definition of perfection. The constant dog-whistle of not being good enough – read 'slim enough', read 'perfect enough' – forms part of the almost subliminal white-noise of self-admonition heard constantly by many men and women, reminding them of their own failings and inadequacy. No one is exempt from some degree of negative self-judgement about their body as the bar of perfection is out of any normal human being's reach. This not-being-good-enough influences everyone to varying degrees, and, as well as colouring how most people judge themselves, it also inevitably affects how they relate to food.

It is impossible not to have made some emotional connection with food as we grow from a dependent, vulnerable baby through to the beginnings of self-definition in adolescence, and into the autonomy of adulthood. Food is an enjoyable, vital source of sustenance for every human. It is impossible to grow and thrive without proper nourishment. Food and eating become complicated for many people when they become something other than an aspect of being alive and well. Social, cultural and psychological constructs influence everyone, and not all these influences encourage a healthy relationship between oneself and food. The effects on each individual are unique.

The degree to which negative versus positive emotions are triggered around food and eating is a key factor in whether a person develops emotional eating issues. Another factor is the extent to which a developing person is allowed to express their emotions within their family. Families that do not permit their offspring to express uncomfortable emotions – such as anger or sadness – often demonstrate in non-verbal ways that those emotions are unwanted, perhaps even shameful. Children learn ways to compensate for not being heard, and may turn to food as a coping mechanism to swallow down, or cover over, their true emotions. Other scenarios where food is used as a tool of control, or reward, can sow the seeds for an emotional response to food in future life. So too can memories of growing up in a chaotic household where the provision of food was erratic or inadequate.

A recent scientific paper presented by clinical psychologist Johnathan Egan, at the 2014 annual conference of the Psychological Society of Ireland, discussed how research showed parental behaviour can have a lifelong effect on a child's relationship with food. The research looked at a group of 550 individuals, most of whom were women. It highlighted that the daughters of strict parents who put their own needs first ahead of those of their children had a higher incidence of emotional or comfort eating, and were typically most likely to gain excess weight in the long term. The daughters of easy-going, liberal parents fared somewhat better. The most favourable outcome for the women – having the lowest levels of emotional eating and correspondingly lower body mass index (BMI) – was found in those with a strict but responsive mother and an easy-going father.

In the work that we, the authors, have undertaken we have become aware of a link between emotional eating and the mother of the household being emotionally absent in some cases. It is worth noting that emotional absence is completely different from physical absence. A working mother who leaves her children each day so as to work away from the home is not necessarily increasing her children's chances of emotional or comfort eating. If the working mother has an adequate emotional connection with her children when she is at home, her offspring can expect to have similarly positive outcomes to if she had been a stay-at-home mum.

Young children learn in non-verbal ways if their mother is withdrawn through depression or mental illness; or is emotionally immature herself and egotistically puts her own needs above theirs; or if her behaviour is chaotic and her emotional absence is due to drug addiction or alcohol abuse; or if she lives under the constant threat of sexual or violent behaviour. These, and similar situations of maternal emotional absence, can block children's natural search for care as they observe their world to be fragile and unsafe. They learn not to express their emotions, to withdraw, and to use food as a way to sooth themselves, literally swallowing down their emotions.

Non-emotional eaters

There are people out there in the wide world who generally eat what they like and, remarkable as it may sound, are not racked with self-loathing or guilt. Feeling relaxed about food means these very same people pay little mind to what they ate at their last meal; nor for that matter do they agonise over what they will eat at the next one. These people have developed few negative triggers around food and view eating as just one of life's many and varied pleasures. They feel little or no concern when considering the prospect of being invited to a celebratory party with a lavish gourmet buffet; they even relish the prospect of a fancy restaurant meal with friends; they don't even baulk at the idea of eating together with their extended family. Their calm take-it-or-leave-it attitude towards food magically keeps their minds liberated to muse on things other than food in their lives, such as their hopes and aspirations, their career, their interests and their loved ones.

It will come as no surprise that these men and women are not our client group. The clients who seek out our therapeutic approach to stopping emotional eating make almost constant negative judgements about themselves in the context of their eating and what their bodies look like. These negative judgements, and the effect of these on their self-esteem, morale, and ability to accept themselves, are what set them apart from non-emotional eaters.

Emotional eaters

There is no single definition of a typical emotional eater. It's a common misconception that all emotional eaters are overweight. Many are within normal weight range but only because of their obsessive dieting, bingeing and disordered eating that will be a well-kept secret they share with no one.

The same negative judgements emotional eaters make about themselves are common to the overweight and the obese, and the dangerously underweight for that matter. All share the trait of unrelenting over-thinking about food coupled with harsh, critical self-judgements.

To give you a sense of a typical emotional eater you need to understand that their innate sense of self-worth – how they actually see themselves as a worthy person – is closely linked to the numbers on their bathroom scales. A pound lost, or a pound gained, can set the tenor of their entire day. Also, foods are never neutral. They are forensically studied and determined to be good or bad.

Emotional eaters battle with their own body's hunger and cravings. They know there have been times when they have succumbed and eaten one 'bad' food only for it to start a tsunami of overeating, or even bingeing and purging, with all the accompanying feelings of shame and self-loathing. An emotional eater's attitude towards him/herself and food is not logical. The extent of his/her preoccupation with food and body weight is often a private source of great personal distress and shame. The reasons for this all-consuming link between food, body weight, self-definition, and how the individual feels about being him/herself in the world, are varied and inevitably complex.

Defined by their weight

Non-emotional eaters also come in all physical shapes and sizes. Some may decide they are heavier than they would like to be. This realisation may come to them gradually over an extended period or more suddenly, as they think about wanting to look their best for a wedding or graduation, or a special birthday or some other milestone life-event. Around this point they now have two main choices – to lose their excess weight or to accept themselves as they are.

For non-emotional eaters who decide to lose some weight, this would mean making appropriate changes and adjustments to their food choices

5

and portion sizes, and maybe even incorporating regular exercise in their routine, until they have reached their goal weight. Unlike emotional eaters, non-emotional eaters do not define themselves completely by how much they weigh or what they look like. Therefore, for them losing weight is no more of a challenge than any other aspect of their lives, such as learning conversational French or taking up water-colours as a hobby. They often successfully lose weight, and even if they do eventually pile on some extra pounds they have the option of just applying their tried-and-trusted methods until they are at their goal weight again.

For non-emotional eaters who decide to stay as they are, being over-weight is not an important issue. Having had the wake-up call that their 'love handles' have become grab rails, they may realise that their weight doesn't really bother them enough to do much about it. It makes it easier to accept their expanding waist lines and bigger clothes sizes when most people they know are, similarly, expanding versions of their former selves. They may consider it hard to feel their weight gain is all that important when the trend of increasing pounds is a familiar trait with their partner, members of their family and friends. They simply get used to buying a size or two larger in their clothes, let out their belts another notch and ultimately pay it little mind.

Obesogenic environment

In many ways there has never been a time when it has been more normal to be overweight. Recent government figures confirm what most people already know from reading the newspapers, watching the news or simply observing larger-sized people wherever they go. Statistics indicate that in the UK over 66 per cent of adult men and over 57 per cent of adult women are overweight or obese. Figures for the USA continue to increase so that at the time of writing just over 71 per cent of all men, and just under 66 per cent of all women, are classed as obese.[1] USA research also shows that in the last decade the heaviest Americans have become even heavier.[2]

The experts' definition of an 'obesogenic' environment (one that promotes significant weight gain) is one where many disparate factors come together to encourage people to eat unhealthily and lead mainly sedentary lives. Predictably, cities are prime examples of an obesogenic environment, inevitably making it more common-place to be overweight: urban living encourages the use of a car over walking, and the multitude of cheap, calorie-dense takeaways along every high street puts temptation within the reach of many whatever the time of day or night.

There are key factors that make emotional eating, and disordered eating in general, more complex than any other type of compulsive behaviour. If someone feels out of control and powerless to resist gambling, smoking, alcohol or drugs, they can be helped therapeutically to end their compulsive behaviour. The measure of success in these cases is often complete cessation of that behaviour. However, when the compulsive behaviour is around food, the person cannot simply stop eating – everyone needs to eat. True success in stopping emotional eating means achieving a healthy integration of food into one's life, possibly for the first time ever. The measure of success here is to arrive at a difference in thinking and self-belief so that it is possible to be calm and relaxed around food, once and for all stepping off the merry-go-round of obsessive over-thinking and critical self-judgement.

Therapy approach

The men and women who self-diagnose themselves as emotional eaters care very much about how much they weigh. However, they are also tired of having so much of their waking time consumed with thoughts of food. Weight loss can be an initial goal for an emotional eater but what they also want in equal measure is to 'feel normal' around food. They want to find a way to turn off their obsessive thinking and to stop berating and hating themselves for every mouthful they eat. They often feel overwhelmed and incapable of making the necessary changes in their thinking about themselves without professional guidance.

Over the last decade, we, the authors, have worked almost exclusively with clients who identify themselves as emotional eaters. Although working independently in our own private practices, we have communicated regularly to share ideas about good practice and insights into successful therapeutic approaches. It was from sharing our successful approaches to stopping emotional eating that we first decided to launch a series of weight-loss workshops in London, focusing on the emotional reasons for overeating. These early (2005) workshops were among the first to use alternative therapies to focus on resolving and releasing the often negative emotions that cause compulsive eating, cravings and self-sabotaging behaviour around food.

Therapy tools

Over the years we have honed our approach and this book is a distillation of everything we have learned working in groups, and one-to-one, with clients who experience the challenges of emotional eating. We are confident we have developed a highly effective set of therapy tools so that people can lose weight appropriately, successfully maintain a healthy weight and, most importantly, feel calm and comfortable around food.

This book describes the therapy tools we have found most effective in stopping emotional eating. These are 'emotional freedom technique' (EFT) (see page 21), percussive suggestion technique (PSTEC) (see page 39) and hypnotherapy, singly and in combination. (The first two may well not be familiar to you and your understanding of the third may well not correspond with what you will discover here (see page 47).) For each individual, the situation is different: some clients may recall specific events or memories that made them think negatively about themselves, most commonly in childhood or adolescence; others may not have any sense of what initially triggered their emotional eating habits. It is not essential to know why the emotional eating began as the therapy focuses on how clients feel about themselves in the here and now.

The therapy tools can be used to reframe or adjust a person's usual negative thoughts about themselves as the first step towards self-forgiveness and self-acceptance. Self-acceptance doesn't mean giving up. It is, however, a vital step in ending harsh, critical self-judgements and exhausting self-blame.

All the therapy tools are described in detail in the book and can be easily learned and applied to dealing with whatever life has in store. Everyone working through the *Seven Steps to Stop Emotional Eating* will approach this book from their own unique perspective. However, we are confident we have provided an easy-to-follow route through the emotional maze towards feeling calm around food and eating for nourishment instead of self-punishment.

As we have said, the therapy tools we have found to be the most effective are hypnotherapy, EFT and PSTEC. Although therapists regularly use one, or sometimes two, of these therapies in combination, we have created our unique approach using all three tools, applying each for its specific strengths, to resolve emotional eating. We have seen the life-changing results from our face-to-face work with clients and have put our knowledge and insights into creating the simple-to-follow self-help format described here.

In-depth information about, and the backgrounds to, each of the therapy tools is given later in the book. However, we acknowledge our first challenge when beginning work with a new client is overcoming their understandable scepticism about what can seem weird and outlandish.

To the uninitiated, EFT probably seems the strangest of all the three therapies as it involves following a pattern of tapping with fingertips on parts of the face and upper body while repeating a spoken phrase. We grant it does seem odd. However, it actually has a proud history in America of helping countless Vietnam military veterans overcome chronic post-traumatic stress disorder (PTSD), and it remains a successful and increasingly well-documented intervention for the troops in contemporary theatres of war.[3, 4, 5]

We use EFT to help clients get in touch with suppressed emotions that are blocking them from achieving what they desire. The EFT process helps to encourage a client's own intuitive insight. From this process clients gain a greater awareness of some of the negative feelings that have been driving their emotional eating. Gaining awareness is an important step to being able to resolve those negative emotions.

With this new-found awareness, PSTEC – the most recently created modality of the three we use – is then used to reduce or erase negative emotions attached to thoughts or memories so that clients can be free of triggers from their past that would have previously led them to self-sabotage their progress. Of the remaining therapy tools, hypnosis is probably the most misunderstood. Most people's opinion of it has been gleaned from watching TV shows where a charismatic entertainer mesmerises volunteers from the audience. The dramatic inductions and trance-like states achieved in the blink of an eye transform ordinary folk into automatons barking like a dog or clucking like a chicken. Hypnosis delivered in a therapy setting could not be more different – it is about inducing a state of complete relaxation that will allow the acceptance of new ideas.

We use hypnosis to support and reinforce all the positive changes being made.

We have made the therapy tools we recommend as easy to learn and use as possible, with printer-friendly worksheets to support the process where appropriate. We have also included links to free audio recordings, to be downloaded and listened to regularly.

We want you to know that our Seven Simple Steps process isn't arduous and can be surprisingly enjoyable. Many people have felt literally weighed down by negativity about themselves for such a long time they have found it a very uplifting process to take the steps to feel lighter and happier in themselves. We have learned through many thousands of hours working with clients that emotional eating is never about being greedy, and never about food. That's why diets don't work, and even bariatric surgery isn't guaranteed to deliver successful weight loss in every case. Hard-won weight losses inevitably turn into weight gains if the underlying reasons for emotional eating are not fully resolved and released. Our approach encourages listening to oneself, and bearing witness with oneself to end critical self-judgements, so that the negative emotions that drove emotional eating can finally stop.

Why this book is needed

If losing weight were only a matter of balancing calories in versus calories out, or cutting down on eating while exercising more, then everyone would simply achieve their natural weight and stay there forever. This is clearly not the case for many people who have struggled with food and weight issues for most of their lives. The simplification that people are overweight because they have no willpower or are greedy ignores the subconscious reasons that compel many people to overeat.

Anorexia and bulimia are already recognised medically, and socially, as eating disorders. Kathy Leach, in her book *The Overweight Patient: A Psychological Approach to Understanding and Working with Obesity*,* explains that these behaviours are acknowledged as coping strategies that most often occur between early childhood and adolescence in response to psychological, environmental and social factors. Obsessive behaviour around food provides a partial sense of control when the individual mainly feels powerless and overwhelmed in other areas of their lives.

Leach continues to observe that overeating and obesity are not so commonly regarded in this way. She states that in her clinical experience, staying overweight and overeating are 'survival decisions'. That is to say, the individual has a subconscious belief (until brought into awareness) that he/she will not survive unless he/she overeats or remains obese.

In our therapeutic experience, weight gain and obesity are the conspicuous byproducts of using food as a strategy to deal with uncomfortable emotions, either to avoid feelings of inner pain, or to block out feelings of boredom, dissatisfaction, anger, sadness or loss.

For some people, the idea of being slim feels like an impossible prospect. Although they often judge themselves harshly for being overweight, they

The Overweight Patient: A Psychological Approach to Understanding and Working with Obesity. Author Kathy Leach. Published by Jessica Kingley 2006, United Kingdom.

remain stuck. Their conscious resolve to lose weight is at odds with – and overruled by – unconscious fears, and limiting beliefs.

For some overweight people, recollections of being slim trigger memories of trauma, or of personal unhappiness that occurred around that time. Considering losing weight can – on a deeply subconscious level – make them feel insecure and at risk all over again.

These fears can be so deeply entrenched that the individual will unconsciously self-sabotage his/her own weight loss to keep him/herself 'safe'. This is typified in yo-yo dieting: successful weight loss isn't maintained but is followed by weight gain followed by further efforts to lose weight – a repeated pattern of behaviour.

Returning again to Kathy Leach, she explains in her book what the goal of therapy is: 'Ultimately, the person struggling with weight issues needs to establish a sense of self-worth, self-esteem, self-love and self-validation, and from this position can decide whether she/he will lose weight, or not. The psychotherapeutic goal is autonomy and empowerment.'

Simple Steps to Stop Emotional Eating sets out how you can discover for yourself the reasons for your own emotional eating so that they can be resolved and released. The book is a written version of the therapy approach we have developed, both together and separately, to work with clients to explore the subconscious, and reveal often hidden benefits from staying overweight.

In place of fear and frustration, we will encourage you in these processes to find new and creative ways of taking care of yourself that do not rely on you swallowing down your emotions with food.

We believe that then, and only then, will you allow yourself to be slim and stay that way, happily and safely, forever.

How to succeed in seven simple steps

Seven Simple Steps to Stop Emotional Eating shows you how to target your body by changing your mind. What that means is that you will:

- Discover and learn for yourself tried and tested therapy tools.
- Learn to distinguish emotional hunger from real hunger.
- Achieve successful, and sustainable, weight loss.
- Resolve your subconscious reasons for emotional eating so that you are free to eat for nourishment.
- End sugar cravings.
- Increase your energy levels.
- Raise your self-esteem through self-acceptance.
- End old patterns of self-sabotage around food.
- Increase your desire to eat only nutritionally healthy food.
- Boost your metabolism.

The book is based on how we work with clients in our own individual practices. It is written in seven simple steps to reflect how we structure our work.

When we work with clients we usually see them weekly for around six or seven weeks, so we feel, as a guide, it would be appropriate if you allowed yourself at least that amount of time to work through the seven steps in this book. Imagine how, by taking no more than an hour or so one evening a week, you can do work that is powerful enough to make a real and lasting difference to your life. That has to be worth fitting into your schedule, however busy you are.

Extending the seven simple steps process over several weeks allows you to process the changes in how you think and feel about yourself, and about food. However, there are no hard and fast rules except that it would be advantageous not to rush yourself, or hurry your work. Some of your habits and thoughts have been with you for a long time and will need some gentle attention to dismantle and release.

Be kind to yourself. If you feel blocked on an issue, then break it down into smaller aspects. We will show you how to do this later in the book when we explain how to apply the therapeutic tools we use (see page 51).

Give yourself the best chance of success by avoiding beginning the seven simple steps process when you are extra busy or stressed, at work or at home, or if you are unusually busy with a spate of social engagements. We want you to have the time to prioritise yourself and to embed positive changes in your behaviour and thoughts that will allow you to take care of yourself in new and improved ways.

Try to resist weighing yourself more than once a week. Just choose a day and stick to it. This is about losing your excess weight for the last time, about you bringing your life back into balance; your weight loss and increased sense of wellbeing will therefore reflect that as you release the emotional drivers behind your emotional eating.

In any one of our client sessions we often use several of the therapy tools featured here. We choose how to work from what naturally arises during the session, and we suggest that you approach your own work in the same way. If one of the therapy tools does not resonate with you, then focus on some of the other tools instead.

We encourage you to begin at Step One and work through to Step Seven so that you can comprehensively address all the factors in, and aspects of, your emotional eating. However, we also acknowledge that you might be tempted to dip in and out, as topics catch your imagination. You can successfully achieve shifts with either approach, but we do recommend you take the time to familiarise yourself with the therapy tools in Part One at the outset. This is so that as you explore your emotions you will have ways to resolve and release old, negative memories and events so that they no longer trigger you to eat, or bother you.

You will learn:

- Emotional Freedom Techniques (EFT) – we are both Advanced

Practitioners of this therapy tool, which will help you to get in touch with your unacknowledged reasons for overeating and to begin the process of releasing and resolving them.

- Percussive Suggestion Technique (PSTEC) – we are both Master Practitioners of this tool, which will help you to reduce or break the emotional connection to an event or memory, so that you are no longer triggered by negative events from the past or things you imagine might happen in the future.
- Hypnotherapy – this will help you to untangle your emotional attachments to food and support all the positive changes you are making with EFT and/or PSTEC, just as it has done with the hundreds of clients we've seen individually in our practices. (We are both qualified hypnotherapists.)

You will discover how old eating habits that no longer serve you can be gently released and effortlessly discarded.

The seven simple steps include three powerful hypnotherapy recordings so that you can harness this wonderful modality to support changes in your behaviour and thinking by speaking directly to your subconscious mind. Other therapeutic modalities included in the programme include:

- the power of **visualisation** – the secret for successful weight loss;
- **Afformations** (see page 142) instead of 'Affirmations' – a subtle yet empowering difference; as well as
- how the **law of attraction** can help you create exactly what you want, both physically and emotionally.

There are worksheets within the book with space dedicated for working out your thoughts and feelings as you disentangle and unfurl the different aspects of your own emotional eating. There is also a pdf version of the worksheets for you to download (see Resources, page 183) and print if you prefer.

Before you begin this process we suggest you dedicate a carefully chosen notebook just for this work, and keep it close to hand. Write at the beginning your goal weight, goal dress size, or goal trouser-waist measurement. Use whatever scale of measurement most resonates with you.

The point of this is to make a declaration. Over time the desire for weight loss can become shrouded in disappointment and frustration, especially when previous failed attempts stand in your way of fully committing to your goal. It is as if failure is simply inevitable. The act of writing your desired goal is to make a stand – a declaration of your intent. You make this stand by setting a clear goal, and your goal needs to have a date by which you will achieve it. Anthony Robbins, the world-famous life coach, said any goal without a date is merely a dream.

Set yourself a goal for the first month, then the weight you want to be one year on. Set incremental steps for your weight loss depending on how much weight you want to lose.

In your mind, plan and plot how you will look and feel and what you will wear on your next birthday, next Easter, at Christmas, at your friend's wedding, and so on. This process is called 'scaffolding', and it becomes the tangible evidence of your intention.

Attach old photographs of yourself when you were the size you want to be. If those photographs do not exist, or are not accessible, then cut out pictures from magazines of body shapes and types you admire.

Feed your imagination with images of what you want for yourself. Strengthen your scaffolding by including lots of photographs: tear sheets from magazines of the clothes, shoes and jewellery you will wear at your goal weight, or size; include pictures of the holiday places you want to visit and of the sort of enjoyable leisure activities you want to do. Perhaps you can remember some of the things you used to enjoy taking part in, but stopped doing years ago? All of this adds clear intent to your subconscious mind so that it knows exactly what you most desire.

Set down your intentions clearly in your notebook. Write yourself a letter from the vantage point of having achieved your goal weight or size. In the letter tell yourself how proud you feel to have achieved your heart's desire. Forgive yourself for not taking care of yourself in the past. Perhaps explain how difficult life has been. Reassure yourself of how much you value *you*, and how you are determined to take better care of yourself in the future. Send love, and forgiveness from your future self back to you, the person beginning your weight-loss journey.

Part One

All the therapy tools you need

Imagine for a moment never achieving what you want and only ever experiencing the opposite. How does that look to you? How does it make you feel? Be assured, changes can happen at the speed of your persistence and commitment to exploring and trying out for yourself the therapy tools in this book.

The therapy tools we use with our clients – Emotional Freedom Technique (EFT), Percussive Suggestion Technique (PSTEC) and hypnotherapy – are all fully explained here so that you can easily learn them and use them to do many important things – change how you think about yourself; re-examine your long-term self-limiting beliefs; encourage clarity; and help you focus on what you really want for yourself. In *Seven Simple Steps to Stop Emotional Eating* the focus is on your relationship with food; however, these very same techniques can be applied to all other areas of your life too. So, when you learn these techniques you will have tools for life, and for whatever life throws at you.

At all times remember, the answer is always in ourselves – we are the answer.

Emotional Freedom Technique

Introducing emotional freedom technique (EFT)

Emotional freedom technique (EFT) is an incredible tool that has been used for over 20 years to help people quickly and effectively overcome a wide variety of physical and emotional issues. Sometimes called 'tapping', it involves actually tapping with two fingers, in a set sequence, on certain predetermined points on your face and upper body. The process itself is different from most other therapy techniques so may seem a little odd at first to newcomers. That's quite a usual reaction so we have provided you with an introduction to this technique with an EFT sequence for increasing the depth of your breathing on page 30. We also fully explain the 'Tapping' sequence on page 25. It is possible when you are out, or in company, that you can release stress and tension by simply imagining yourself working through the tapping points illustrated there.

Developed in the USA by Gary Craig in the early 1990s, EFT has developed into his lifelong passion even though he was neither a licensed therapist nor a trained psychologist – he was actually a Stanford-trained engineer.

Many of the underlying principles of EFT came from Craig's training in a discipline called 'Thought Field Therapy' (TFT – see below) under the tutorship of psychologist, Dr Roger Callahan.

The history of EFT is fascinating. Its origins lie in traditional Chinese Medicine, including acupuncture, which has been the primary form of medicine in China for more than 5000 years. Recent research has confirmed the flow of energy (Qi) along invisible meridians, or pathways, in the body.

Acupuncture was originally developed to treat physical problems, although today practitioners frequently use it also to treat anxiety and stress.

Dr George Goodheart, a chiropractor in the US, developed an interest in acupuncture, and went on to introduce a new method into his practice called 'applied kinesiology', which is a form of muscle testing. He achieved the same results as acupuncture by tapping on the acupuncture points. Australian psychiatrist, John Diamond MD, then went on to create another variant of this wherein he had the client tapping on the same points, and repeating positive affirmations to treat any emotional symptoms.

Dr Roger Callahan went further to find that by tapping certain algorithms, or particular patterns, or tapping sequences, his patients were able to release specific anxieties, or phobias, and the first meridian tapping patterns were created. If a client concentrated on a problem, or fear, and tapped at the same time, following a specific pattern, then the issue could be resolved, in some cases permanently. Thought Field Therapy (TFT) was born.

Later it occurred to Gary Craig, who had studied TFT extensively with Callahan, that a single algorithm, or pattern of tapping, might work just as well. Craig went on to develop his own individual single algorithm which he called 'Emotional Freedom Technique' (EFT).

EFT is now the most influential and widely known Energy Psychology method in the world. It has been used successfully in treatments for an incredibly wide variety of issues, including fears, anxieties, phobias and post-traumatic stress disorder, just to mention a few. [7, 8, 9] EFT has also proved to be very successful as a technique for managing, or reducing the impact, and/ or frequency of, physical issues, such as migraines, tinnitus, IBS (irritable bowel syndrome), fibromyalgia and TN (trigeminal neuropathic facial nerve pain), to name but a few examples.

It is an easy enough technique to be mastered by most people, and you don't have to believe in meridian energy pathways in the body for it to work.

Learn how to work successfully with EFT

To get started you need to turn off your phone and ensure that you have around 30 minutes in which you will not be disturbed. It would be helpful to familiarise yourself with all the 'tapping points' you may need to use. It's easy to follow these in our diagram (see Figure 1).

You should then follow the steps that are outlined below.

As you become more adept, and learn to trust your own instincts more, you will find you'll be able to naturally and intuitively compose your own EFT setups, and find your own words to say as you tap around on each point. Your own words are always more powerful as they are customised to your own requirements, and then you will really feel how powerful and life-changing EFT can be for you.

Preparation

Before you start tapping you should:
1. Familiarise yourself with all the tapping points, as shown in Figure 1.
2. Choose the emotional event or memory that you wish to work on, making sure to start with something you know you can manage emotionally (see Note below).
3. Determine the negative emotion attached to the problem that you are focusing on. The easiest way to do this is by setting a number, or score, to assess the negative emotional intensity attached to whatever issue you are addressing. Therapists tend to call this a 'SUD rating'. That means 'subjective units of discomfort'. Zero would mean there is no emotion attached to a memory, or an event, and 10 would be the biggest emotion you can feel.
4. Focus on the issue you have chosen to address. So, what is your SUD rating? Take your time. Consider where you feel those emotions in your body. If the emotions you are feeling had a colour, or a shape, or a texture, what would that be? Give yourself time to really focus on that emotion and then take an intuitive guess at your SUD rating and make a note of it.

Note: An important word of guidance – as we have said, begin with an emotional event, or memory, that you are sure you can manage emotionally. Choose to practise, building your confidence and expertise with EFT, on issues with low SUD ratings (for example, try 'EFT for sceptics' below). If you feel the need to deal with something more traumatic, with a higher SUD rating, it may be advisable to break it down into smaller parts, or aspects, so that you can keep yourself emotionally safe and not become overwhelmed. An example of tackling aspects of an issue to make sure it is not emotionally overwhelming would be to focus on less significant examples of the negative emotion you are addressing. For instance, if you feel huge negative emotion attached to a traumatic event or memory, it would be advisable to select a minor uncomfortable incident or occasion associated with a similar negative emotion and reduce the SUD rating first on that. You can incrementally move up the SUD scale as your confidence in your own resilience grows so that at all times you are keeping yourself emotionally safe. Alternatively, work with a qualified meridian energy therapist.

The EFT set-up
Once you have your SUD rating, what is called the 'set-up' (essentially, mental preparation) takes place while either rubbing on what is called the 'sore spot' (that is the place on your chest where you would pin a brooch or a medal) or by tapping the fingertips of one hand against the Karate-chop side of the other hand (that's the part of your hand you would use if you were Karate chopping a piece of wood).

The 'set-up' focuses the conscious mind on the task in hand, so take your time with this. Really listen to what you are saying to yourself, and how it feels.

It doesn't matter if you tap with your right hand on your left hand, or left hand on your right hand. As you tap, say the following out loud:

> 'Even though I have this [insert problem or feeling here], I completely, and fully, love and accept myself, and forgive myself.'

You should repeat the set-up three times.

Tapping
You are now ready to begin tapping. Generally use two fingers of your dominant hand, together, to tap seven or eight times on each point shown in

EFT TAPPING POINTS

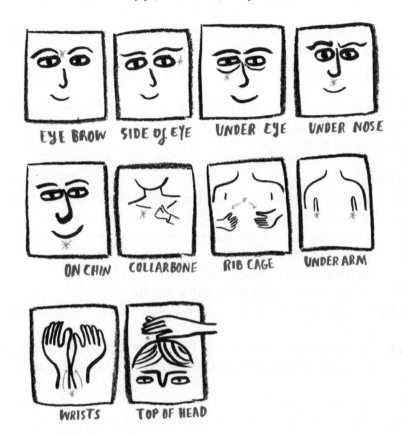

EYE BROW   SIDE OF EYE   UNDER EYE   UNDER NOSE

ON CHIN   COLLARBONE   RIB CAGE   UNDER ARM

WRISTS   TOP OF HEAD

Figure 1: The EFT tapping points are:
1. **Eyebrow (EB)** At the inner end of one eyebrow, level with the top of your nose.
2. **Side of eye (SE)** Side of the eye, at the end of your eyebrow.
3. **Under eye (UE)** Under the eye, on the curved bone of your eye socket.
4. **Under nose (N)** In the dip under your nose.
5. **On chin (C)** In the dip under the bottom lip, on your chin.
6. **Collarbone (CB)** Around your collarbone (with a soft fist).
7. **Ribcage (RIBS)** Fingers of both hands tapping on your ribcage at both sides of your body.
8. **Under arm (UA)** Flat hand at the side of your body, level with a woman's bra strap or a man's nipple, about 4 inches (10 cm) down from under your arm.
9. **Wrists (W)** Tap the insides of your wrists together.
10. **Top of head (TH)** Tap around with a flat hand on top of your head.

Figure 1 and listed below before moving on. There is no need to count the number of taps precisely, but be sure to tap with enough pressure to feel a slight bounce.

As you tap around each meridian point, repeat a reminder phrase – for example, 'This chocolate craving', or 'This sadness', or 'This emptiness' or 'This anger in my belly'.

The tapping points are:
1. **EB** At the inner end of one eyebrow, level with the top of your nose.
2. **SE** Side of the eye, at the end of your eyebrow.
3. **UE** Under the eye, on the curved bone of your eye socket.
4. **N** In the dip under your nose.
5. **C** In the dip under the bottom lip on your chin.
6. **CB** Around your collarbone (with a soft fist).
7. **RIBS** Fingers of both hands tapping on your rib cage at both sides of your body.
8. **UA** Flat hand at the side of your body, level with a woman's bra strap or a man's nipple, about 4 inches (10 cm) down from under your arm.
9. **W** Tap the insides of your wrists together.
10. **TH** Tap around with a flat hand on top of your head.

Each round should take only about 30-40 seconds to perform.

After a tapping round, take a deep breath in, followed by a slow breath out. Sip some water. Good hydration is recommended with all energy work.

Now, check your SUD rating. Has it gone up or down? Have other things come to your mind?

You may need to tap for another couple of complete rounds. The aim is to continue until you have successfully reduced the SUD rating to a low number, or zero. Use your notebook to jot down any other aspects of your issue that may have come to your mind while you have been tapping, but stay focused on what you began with. Insights you write down are for future rounds of EFT.

If many different thoughts or emotions jostle for attention, these are probably the different aspects, or associated parts, of the issue you are working on. If you are not sure where next to direct your EFT work, then it's a good idea to write down those thoughts and emotions and give each one a SUD rating. Keep within the SUD range you feel capable of dealing with. It's your responsibility here to keep yourself emotionally safe while working on your issues.

To download the A4 printer-friendly EFT aide memoire PDF go to www. your7simplesteps.com and click on the EFT tab.

Are you feeling sceptical about 'tapping'?

As we mentioned in the Introduction, EFT can look very odd to the uninitiated, so for all the sceptics out there who are really wondering how tapping on their face can help with their emotional eating issues – the next EFT script is for you. This will have the positive benefit of introducing you to the technique, and allowing you to practise on an issue that is not emotionally charged in the way bad memories may be.

Stage 1: Establish your SUD rating for scepticism!
Rate your level of scepticism on a scale of zero to 10, with 10 equal to being completely disbelieving and zero equal to your being completely open to EFT helping you.

Stage 2: EFT set-up for the first tapping round
Here's approximately what you say to yourself, preferably out loud, as you tap with the fingertips of one hand on your 'sore spot' or the Karate-chop side of the other hand. (As we will say many times in this book, words you have scripted for yourself are always actually more powerful so our words are just a rough guide to get you started):

'Even though I'm doubting that this tapping thing can work for me, I, completely and fully love and accept myself.'

'Even though this tapping stuff looks too silly and hippy-dippy and it can't possibly work, I completely and fully love and accept myself as I am now.'

'Even though I don't believe that tapping on my face can possibly work for me as my issues are too deep, I completely and fully love and accept myself without judgement.'

Stage 3: First round of tapping

Now, here is approximately what you might say as you tap on each of the tapping (meridian) points. Remember the whole round should take you no more than half a minute:

EB: 'This tapping can't possibly work for me.'
SE: 'It's far too hippy-dippy.'
UE: 'It can't be this easy,
N: 'and my issues are far too deep
C: 'to be resolved by tapping on my face.'
CB: 'I have so much doubt
RIBS: 'that tapping could help me at all.'
UA: 'I feel silly even thinking this tapping could help me.'
W: 'My problems won't disappear
TH: 'by just tapping on my face!'

Pause. Take one easy, deep breath.

Stage 4: EFT set-up for the second tapping round

Now, this is approximately what you should say in preparing for the second round of tapping. Remember to tap on either the 'sore' spot or the Karate-chop side of your other hand, and it is best to say the words out loud:

'Even though I still have this doubt that tapping will work for me. I completely and fully love and accept myself.'

'Even though this tapping is far too hippy-dippy, I completely and fully love and accept myself as I am now.'

'Even though I'm still doubting that tapping would even work for me because it looks so strange and I'm embarrassed to even do it, I completely and fully love and accept myself without judgement and I'm open to the possibility of at least trying it.'

Stage 5: Second round of tapping

Now, say words approximating to the following, preferably out loud, as you tap on each meridian point:

EB:	'All these doubts...'
SE:	'It can't possibly work for me.'
UE:	'It looks so stupid
N:	'and I'd be so embarrassed if others saw me doing this.'
C:	'What would they think of me?'
CB:	'I'm open to the possibility of not worrying about what others think
RIBS:	'and letting go of these fears of being judged by others.'
UA:	'I'm open to the possibility of at least trying this tapping
W:	'and seeing if it helps at all.'
TH:	'I'm open to the possibility of tapping helping me to start healing my issues.'

Pause. Take one easy, deep breath.

Check your SUD rating. Has it gone up or down?

Stage 6: EFT set-up for third tapping round

Now say while tapping:

'Even though I'm still not 100 per cent convinced that tapping will work for me, I completely and fully love and accept myself.'

'Even though I am still a little worried about looking silly tapping on my face, I completely and fully love and accept myself as I am now.'

'Even though there's a part of me thinking I look silly doing this, there's a bigger part of me now willing to learn this process and start to resolve my issues.'

Stage 7: Third round of tapping

This time, say words approximating to the following, preferably out loud, as you tap on each meridian point:

EB:	'I'm still not 100 per cent convinced
SE:	'because I know I'll look silly,
UE:	'but I'm willing to at least try now
N:	'and release these fears of being judged.'
C:	'It's OK for me to relax and experiment with this process.'
CB:	'I'm willing to trust that it just might work for me
RIBS:	'and that feels exciting.'
UA:	'I'm willing to allow myself the chance to succeed.'
W:	'I love the thought that I can actually resolve my issues.'
TH:	'I'm allowing myself to feel open, loving and accepting.'

Pause. Take one easy, deep breath.

Now, check your SUD rating for scepticism. If you're still feeling sceptical, you can tap another couple of rounds until you feel more open and excited about allowing yourself to succeed.

EFT demonstrates how stress can affect your breathing

When demonstrating EFT to clients we have found it useful to begin by focusing on something with which the client can tangibly, and pretty quickly, experience some changes. We have found that focusing on breathing works wonderfully for this. We have therefore included our set-up for this for you to practise with as you work with EFT for the first time (or second, if you have tried out 'for sceptics' on page 27).

The depth of our breathing can be an accurate guide to the level of stress we carry in our body on an almost constant basis. Many clients are actually surprised when we ask them to take time to assess the depth of their breathing only to become aware that their breathing is constricted or shallow. Sadly, it's become the norm for them unconsciously to breathe in this way and therefore restrict the physical and psychological benefits of breathing fully and deeply. Life-giving oxygen transported throughout our body is a cornerstone of health and wellbeing. EFT works powerfully and gently to free and expand breathing from the stranglehold of tension and stress.

Stage 1: Establish your rating for breathing

Rate your breathing capacity on a scale of zero to 10, with zero equal to no breath at all and 10 equal to your breathing working at full capacity.

Stage 2: EFT set-up for the first tapping round

Tap the fingers of one hand on your other hand, as described for the set-up above, while saying out loud:

'Even though I'm only breathing at a number... [Say your breathing rate here] and I'm not sure why I'm not breathing as fully as I can, I completely and fully love and accept myself.'

'Even though my shallow breathing represents all sorts of stress that I don't even want to look at, I completely and fully love and accept myself as I am now.'

'Even though my shallow breathing represents all the stress I am carrying in my body, I completely and fully love and accept myself without judgement.'

After saying this, take three fairly deep and gentle breaths. Breathe in through your nose and softly out through the mouth. Don't use any force or pressure.

Now focus for a moment on your breathing and assess the depth of the breaths you have taken.

Stage 3: First round of tapping for breathing

Say words approximating to the following, preferably out loud, as you tap on each meridian point:

EB: 'This shallow breathing'

SE: 'Stress in my body'

UE: 'I'm only breathing at a number... [say your breathing rate here]'

N: 'This represents all kinds of stress I'm carrying'

C: 'I have this shallow breathing'

CB: 'I don't even want to know why'

RIBS: 'All sorts of stress in my body'

UA: 'I'm only breathing at a number... [say your breathing rate here]'

W: 'It represents all the stress I'm carrying'

TH: 'I don't even want to know why'

Pause.
Take one easy, deep breath.

Stage 4: EFT set-up for the second tapping round

This time you should say something on the following lines, preferably out loud:

'Even though I still have this shallow breathing, I choose to breathe deeply and freely and I completely and fully love and accept myself.'

'Even though my shallow breathing represents all sorts of stress I'm carrying in my body, I completely and fully love and accept myself as I am now.'

'Even though I'm only breathing at a...[say your breathing rate here], I choose to breathe out all this stress and allow my body to breathe in deeply and I completely and fully love and accept myself without judgement.'

Stage 5: Second round of tapping for breathing

This time, as you tap on the relevant meridian point, you should say:

EB: 'I choose to breathe deeply.'
SE: 'Releasing this stress from my body.'
UE: 'I ask my body to breathe deeply.'
N: 'Filling my lungs with life-giving oxygen. '
C: 'I choose to breathe deeply.'
CB: 'Releasing this stress from my body.'
RIBS: 'Breathing deeply.'
UA: 'Breathing out stress.'
W: 'Breathing in calmness.'
TH: 'Releasing stress from my body.'.

Pause.
Take one easy, deep breath.
Assess your level of breathing and rate it again from zero to 10.

Stage 6: EFT set-up for third tapping round
Tap the fingers of one hand on your other hand while saying out loud:

'Even though I'm still only breathing at a...[say your breathing rating here], I choose to breathe out stress and allow my body to breathe in calmness and I completely and fully love and accept myself.'

'Even though I am carrying all this stress in my body, I choose to allow myself to breathe deeply and fully and I completely and fully love and accept myself as I am now.'

'Even though my shallow breathing represents all sorts of stuff I don't even want to look at, I allow myself to breathe in calmness and breathe out tension.'

Stage 7: Third round of tapping for breathing
In this third round the statements to make are:

EB: 'Releasing the remaining tightness from my breathing.'
SE: 'Releasing the remaining stress from my body.'
UE: 'Releasing more with every breath.'

N: 'Breathing deeper with every breath.'
C: 'Choosing to breathe deeply and easily.'
CB: 'Releasing the remaining stress from my body.'
RIBS: 'Breathing in forgiveness and peace.'
UA: 'Breathing out stress and tension.'
W: 'Allowing myself to breathe fully.'
TH: 'Filling my lungs with life-giving oxygen.'

Pause. Take one easy, deep breath.
Assess your level of breathing and rate it from zero to 10.

Note: Repeat the first tapping round if required to further increase your breathing rating.

To view a video demonstration of how to increase your breathing with EFT go to www.your7simplesteps.com and click on the EFT tab.

EFT 9 Gamut procedure

EFT 9 Gamut procedure is an additional powerful EFT technique that is useful when dealing with cravings and releasing entrenched compulsive habits and behaviours. It can supercharge your results when using EFT and can be especially effective if you are finding the issues you are tapping on are particularly stubborn or resistant to change.

In addition, if you thought EFT looked strange, then the 9 Gamut can look even more absurd so it's worth taking a moment here to understand exactly why you are being asked to hum, count numbers and move your eyes in a particular way.

The EFT 9 Gamut procedure facilitates a bilateral stimulation of the brain. It works by combining nine individual activities that collectively take less than 10 seconds to perform. These activities alternatively engage the right side of the brain, known in lay-terms as the creative part, and the left side of the brain, again known in lay-terms as the logical, reasoning part of the brain.

This is achieved by performing specific eye movements. One's eyes have a direct connection to the brain via the optic nerve and the specific eye movements are chosen for how they stimulate particular parts of the brain, including memory, internal dialogue and imagination. At the same time, the humming of a musical refrain and the counting out-loud of numbers 1 to 5, switch brain activation from the right hemisphere to the left hemisphere, and back again.

Here's how to do it. Firstly, determine the subjective unit of discomfort (SUD) rating of the issue you are addressing. We explained this concept in our introduction to EFT. It is a simple way of assessing the negative emotional intensity around an issue for you. Zero is no emotional intensity and 10 is the strongest emotional intensity you can feel. Taking a moment to score your emotional distress acts as a useful benchmark as you progress with your work.

1. Firstly, locate the 'Gamut point'. This is the groove you can locate on the back of either hand. Looking at your knuckles, it is an indentation just up on the back of your hand between the knuckles of your ring finger and your little finger, or pinkie.
2. While continually tapping with two fingers of the opposite hand on the Gamut point, carry out each of the following nine steps, keeping your head still throughout:
   1. Close your eyes.
   2. Open your eyes.
   3. Look down hard to the right.
   4. Look down hard to the left.
   5. Smoothly roll your eyes in a full circle clockwise. If this feels difficult, visualise instead following the hands of a clock with your eyes from 12 through to 12 again.
   6. Roll your eyes in a full circle anti-clockwise.
   7. Hum approximately five seconds of any song – 'Happy Birthday' works well, or any other tune you know.
   8. Next count out loud the numbers 1,2,3,4,5.
   9. Hum a few bars again of your chosen tune.

EFT 9 GAMUT PROCEDURE

Figure 2: EFT 9 Gamut procedure

If you are working on an issue that feels particularly difficult to shift we recommend augmenting your EFT work with the 9 Gamut procedure. Try it out as an extension at the end of your standard EFT rounds. Familiarise yourself first with the slightly unusual instructions (page 35) for this procedure as your ability to carry these out accurately will affect its potential to resolve deep-seated issues. Retain your focus with the issue you are working with for best results.

Now, check the SUD rating again on the issue you are working with. If it still has any emotional charge to it, then repeat the complete EFT process again beginning with a round of EFT and finishing with the 9 Gamut procedure.

To download the A4 printer-friendly EFT 9 Gamut procedure aide memoire PDF go to www.your7simplesteps.com and click on the EFT tab.

Work on your own with EFT

Some people get very hung up about what they should say when they tap around on the points. Don't worry. A complete tapping round should only take about 30-40 seconds, so there really is no reason to be precious. Consider it just ad-libbing, or stream of consciousness. There is no right or wrong thing to say with EFT.

Take your time to really be present with your emotions.

To download the A4 printer-friendly EFT composing template pdf go to www.your7simplesteps.com and click on the EFT tab.

Percussive Suggestion Technique

Introducing percussive suggestion technique (PSTEC)

Tim Phizackerley had been a full-time, UK-based hypnotherapist for several years when he created PSTEC (percussive suggestion technique). Previously, he had specialised in various therapeutic areas using hypnosis, including resolving bulimic and anorexic behaviour. It is recognised that these are some of the toughest issues to 'crack' using conventional therapy methods.

Tim developed new techniques to assist him in dealing with these exceptionally demanding issues. This is one reason why he created the 'PSTEC™ audios', which we will explain in a minute.

Before coming to hypnosis, Tim was a professional programmer and computer analyst. While working in the computer programming field, one of his interests was writing computer programs of an artificially intelligent nature for applications such as chess, draughts, or the interpretation of language.

Tim had always been conscious that the human mind is the product of evolutionary processes. At its core lies an organic computer. The one thing which absolutely all computers have in common is that they run programs. As he delved deeper into the mechanisms underlying hypnosis, he recognised certain things about the interaction between the conscious and subconscious mind that he believed could open the door to literally reprogramming the human subconscious computer in new and innovative ways.

At the beginning, Tim never expected to be applying what he knew about artificial intelligence, or computer programming, to working with people, but fate seemed to have hypnotherapy, and hypnosis, in mind for him, along with applications like PSTEC. As it happens, hypnosis, and PSTEC, have played a pivotal role in encouraging a full recovery from a medical crisis of a close member of his family. Since then he has used hypnosis and PSTEC for various emergencies and it has been of tremendous value to his family, as well as his clients.

PSTEC audios combine a variety of existing and well-known psychological principles presented in a highly focused and very specific way. These techniques include 'pattern interrupting' and associative conditioning, and also suggestion. These particular techniques have been extensively studied by psychologists* and all have been previously applied with varying levels of success in a number of therapeutic methodologies. Other therapies, such as cognitive behaviour therapy (CBT) and neuro-linguistic programming (NLP) tend to use only one approach or principle at any given time, whereas PSTEC blends multiple methods in extremely rapid and highly interwoven combinations. The specific mix of these and other components, together with precision timing, careful integration and minute attention to detail in the formulation of the PSTEC audios, is what sets PSTEC apart from other ways of changing beliefs and emotional states.

In simple terms, the intricate composition of the PSTEC audio 'click tracks' provides a very powerful and repetitive delivery of these techniques and a number of others.

As well as suggesting new outcomes, the basic PSTEC click tracks overlay emotionally neutral states on what would have been emotionally charged thoughts, or memories. Because the old automatic responses have been interrupted, the mind is able to quickly accept the new suggested outcomes, and this usually provides a rapid and lasting release from any problem feeling or negative emotion.

* Anyone wishing to know about 'anchors' should read about the Nobel Prize winning research of Ivan Petrovich Pavlov. An anchor is a modern name for the neurological connections he both discovered and studied which relate to conditioned responses. 'Pattern interrupts' interfere with conditioned neurological responses in order to open up new possibilities. They are used widely in NLP. For a reasonably clear explanation of pattern interrupts, Edward de Bono's classic book *Mechanism of Mind* is a good place to begin.

PSTEC is not a passive exercise so it is important to follow the instructions completely. You will be listening to the voice of Tim Phizackerley on the audio tracks together with two click beat tracks, and also a tone track. There is a click beat track for the fingers of your right hand to tap along to and another, different click beat track for the fingers of your left hand to tap along to. Finally, the third track has no clicks; it is simply a tone, and when you hear that you tap along with the fingers of both hands.

Initially, Tim created two free PSTEC click tracks that could be listened to alternatively. The choice of tracks helps to keep the subconscious from becoming too familiar to any one set of tapping instructions so you can use them alternatively, or occasionally switch tracks to add variety.

Many people have used the free click tracks to resolve and release a wide variety of issues with great success. In recent years, Tim has gone on to create and develop additional optional PSTEC tracks, often to address specific issues, as well as PSTEC tracks to embed positive changes. A complete listing with full descriptions is available in the 'PSTEC turbo charge your results' section of this book (see page 44).

> *To download the free PSTEC click tracks go to www.your7simplesteps.com and click on the PSTEC tab.*

Learn how to work successfully with PSTEC

This amazing technique is deceptively simple. The basic free PSTEC click tracks can be used for almost anything. Many people have utilised these tracks to clear tremendous amounts of trauma without having to spend any money at all.

When using PSTEC the important thing to remember is that you need to be 'in the emotion'. Use the SUD scale to check the intensity of the experience and get it as high on the scale as you possibly can. Try getting it up to a 10 out of 10. Remember, when working on your own it is important to consider your mental wellbeing and build up your confidence and resilience by practising using PSTEC on issues that are not emotionally overwhelming. So, begin on less important issues. For instance if you are struggling with an issue with someone who is very important in your life you will need to practise and experiment with PSTEC prior to tackling that issue. Begin perhaps by focusing on a person who is more peripheral in your life. This could be a co-worker; or you could focus on a trivial incidence in a shop or on public transport and work on the emotions that experience engenders first. Run the click track remembering to stay in the emotion as you listen and interact. It is vital to concentrate only on the experience you started with. Tempting as it may be, do not allow your mind to drift off on to any other experiences.

Before you start
Before you start working with PSTEC we suggest you make a list of the issues you have with your body, and with food, that make you uncomfortable. Include any experiences, either old or recent, that may have had an impact on how you view yourself or how you view food.

Here are a few suggestions to prompt you to come up with your own:

- Do you remember being bullied at school and consider it feels safer to be big so that at least you can protect yourself?
- As a child, do you remember not being allowed to have any sweets or treats?
- Do you remember occasions of not having enough to eat when you were young? How do you feel now when you get hungry?
- Can you recall being told that you have to eat everything on your plate, or you can't have dessert?

Choose an experience that feels uncomfortable for you. Ask yourself, 'Does this feel familiar?' If it does, allow your mind to gently drift back to an earlier memory of the same, familiar feeling. Let yourself be there so that you can see what you saw then, and feel what you felt then. You may be able to track that familiar feeling back several times to a very early memory, or perhaps even to the first time you felt those feelings.

Once you are fully there, seeing and feeling those same old, familiar feelings, score it on the SUD scale from zero to 10.

Go to a place where you won't be disturbed. Turn off your phone, and make yourself comfortable. Don't lie down as you might find you drop off to sleep, and that would not be helpful!

Listening to the PSTEC click tracks over headphones is best. The voice-over will talk you through the process at the beginning of the track, giving you all the instructions you need, so make sure you listen to this carefully.

It is a confusing and demanding process, so commit to doing the best you can. Hold the thought or memory that you are working on in your mind.

When the track has finished, revisit the experience in your mind and see how high the intensity is now. Does the SUD scale register a reduction in intensity? Don't be alarmed if it hasn't shifted at all. Although this is very rare, just run the click track through again, ensuring that you are really tapping in to your emotions. It often helps to sip from a glass of water. Continue listening, and interacting with the click tracks until the intensity is down to zero.

It is important to remember that you must not switch your attention to another experience at any time while running the track – just retain your focus and keep working on your experience until it has no emotional charge at all.

Clear out those old negatives memories one by one, and notice how different you begin to feel. You may notice that you're feeling lighter and happier, and in many cases your old eating patterns will start to change for the better.

Please note: 'Reminder statements' are the short phrases you say out loud while tapping each point when working with emotional freedom technique (EFT). When you are working with percussive suggestion technique

(PSTEC) 'reminder statements' should NOT be used since this can be counterproductive for some people. For anyone who feels they really need a reminder to help them stay focused on their issue, then a single word reminder is okay, such as this anger, or this disappointment.

Turbo-charge your results with PSTEC's optional tools

It is possible to undertake an impressive amount of therapeutic work using just the free PSTEC audio tracks. However, there is so much more to the amazing PSTEC process than just the free click tracks. Tim Phizackerley has created additional, powerful, dedicated click tracks to turbo-charge your results, as well as click tracks which focus on specific issues.

Additional click tracks are individually available for a small fee. It is your choice to work with just the free click tracks or to invest in buying optional tracks as you work through your issues. As you begin to recognise the amazing changes you can make with the free PSTEC click tracks, you can choose to add additional tracks to speed your work or embed positive changes.

PSTEC accelerators

The accelerator tracks can make PSTEC work better and even faster. They can stimulate recall so that you are able to clear more problems. They are almost essential for longer-term use to ensure your subconscious does not become familiar with the order of clicks and tones in the two free click tracks.

EEFs – Extra-powerful PSTEC click tracks

Extra-strong click tracks are also available for issues that are particularly resistant to releasing, such as negative feelings or emotions that have been experienced for a long period of time, or have multiple sources. (These tracks are also available as part of the level one package.)

PSTEC level one

This includes additional guidance on how best to work with the PSTEC tracks as well as the 'PSTEC Positive' track to help shift your limiting beliefs and EEF's extra-powerful click tracks too. (Limiting beliefs and how they impact on your life and issues around weight are fully explored later in the book on page 55).

Success with PSTEC and PSTEC Positive

PSTEC positive tracks are the perfect technique to embed specific positive changes into your subconscious mind. (Also available as part of level one package.)

PSTEC cascade release

This technique works extraordinarily well in making emotional shifts to release memories, or events around a specific theme. If there is a strong thematic link to periods of your life, or you notice repetitions of destructive patterns in weight loss and weight gain, then you can turbo charge your results by using one of the optional PSTEC click tracks. PSTEC Cascade Release was created for working with associated events, memories or conclusions you have about yourself that keep you stuck and no longer serve you. It enables you to resolve and release numerous events, or memories, simultaneously around common themes. It works on the subconscious mind completely differently from the other PSTEC tools and so with this technique you'll find you can even work where there are no feelings and no known memories.

An example of this could be working through the patterns of weight gain you experience when in a long-term relationship. It's quite common to gain weight while in a settled relationship and that pattern would be an ideal theme to resolve with PSTEC Cascade Release. You might have many memories of staying in during the evening and how the cooking and eating of food plays an important bonding, or reward/treat-type role in your relationship. Another example of a theme may be around eating and work. Perhaps you often overeat when stressed at work? Again, this pattern of behaviour could be released successfully using this technique. Just use the many memories you have of rushing lunch at your desk or grazing on snacks all afternoon and your subconscious mind will do the rest.

PSTEC positive power

This variant adds extra power to PSTEC Positive and provides essential variety. It is important with all click tracks that your subconscious does not become too familiar with the order of any of the clicks and tones.

PSTEC FAD for ending food and drink cravings

Tim Phizackerley has produced two highly effective click tracks developed to specifically deal with food and drink cravings. They are designed to break addictions to junk foods and sugary drinks. The compulsion to consume these items is replaced with suggestions to eat healthier alternatives.

Go to www.your7simplesteps.com and click on the PSTEC Turbo Charge for a complete listing and description of all the PSTEC optional tools.

Hypnotherapy for positive change

Introducing hypnosis to support positive change

Hypnotherapy is a wonderful way of using hypnosis techniques to resolve a whole range of issues and problems, including stress, pain and childbirth pain. Hypnosis as such doesn't achieve anything of itself: it's what happens when you go into that wonderful, relaxed state that creates the amazing results. It is a highly relaxing experience with no side effects, or after effects.

With hypnotism you cannot be made to do anything against your will, or your moral and ethical standards. It is merely a natural phenomenon that you experience many times during your day – for example, when watching a television programme or reading a good book we all naturally drift in and out of awareness.

Hypnosis results in a wonderfully relaxed state, but you are always in total control. It is not sleep, although if you're listening to the 'audios' we have recorded for you to download (see below) when you're tired you may well find you do drop off to sleep. Think about the changes you want to make. You've probably succeeded for a while in changing eating habits, for instance, but old behaviours eventually come back. This is because you have not addressed the underlying patterns that were causing your behaviour in the first place.

In hypnosis you can easily let those patterns go and replace them with powerful, beneficial suggestions that fully support the new life you aspire to.

Hypnotherapy FAQs

Q: What is hypnotherapy?
A: Hypnotherapy is the therapeutic application of hypnosis as a wonderful tool to support beneficial change. It is used in many

situations, including stress relief, pain management and childbirth. It is the third key therapeutic tool we use with our clients in face-to-face sessions. For this book we have specially recorded three powerful hypnosis sequences that you can download via your computer as MP3s (see page 186). We recommend you listen to one every day while you are focusing on losing weight.Think about your weight-loss goals. You've probably succeeded in losing weight for a while, but the old behaviours eventually come back, don't they? This is because you haven't sorted out the underlying patterns that are causing you to behave this way. With hypnotherapy we are able to help you to easily let those self-sabotaging patterns of behaviour go, and support your successful weight loss with new positive ways of thinking and feeling about yourself.

Q: What must I do before listening to the hypnosis audio tracks?
A: Find a quiet place where you are able to relax without interruption. All the audio tracks are less than 20 minutes long. If possible, turn off the telephone, dim the lights or draw the curtains.

Q: Are there some people who can't be hypnotised?
A: No. It's a natural process. Anyone who can follow simple instructions can be hypnotised.

Q: What if I go to sleep?
A: It's fine. If you do doze off while listening to the hypnotherapy audio tracks, the positive suggestions will still go deeply into your subconscious mind and changes can take place. Equally, if you are unexpectedly required to return to full awareness while listening to the audio tracks, you will be alert and feel fully awake, without any grogginess.

Q: What will it feel like?
A:There is no such thing as a hypnotised feeling. In hypnosis, you will feel exactly the same as you would if you were engrossed in a book or absorbed in an interesting movie. It is simply a very relaxed feeling that most people truly enjoy, and sometimes wish they didn't have to leave behind.

Q: Will I lose control listening to these audios?
A: No. You are always completely in control of your body, and thoughts. Hypnosis is absolutely safe and has been used for a long time by dentists, doctors and psychotherapists. It is a proven therapeutic aid.

Q: How does hypnosis help with weight loss?
A: When you are in a lovely relaxed state, your mind is much more receptive to positive suggestions. It then goes on to make the desired changes that you are seeking. When you're listening to the audios we encourage you to use the power of your imagination. We talk more about this in the section on visualisation (see page 97).

The Seven Simple Steps hypnotherapy audios

We have provided three specific, professionally recorded MP3 audios to assist your successful weight loss. You can download these tracks to your computer or smart phone. At around 20 minutes or less, you can listen through headphones whenever you have time to relax. You can even listen to the recordings as an audio loop while you sleep at night. The hypnotic words will go deep into your subconscious mind and support all the positive changes you are making in your life.

Hypnosis to shrink your stomach

The power of suggestion can help you to feel fuller more quickly. Use the power of your mind to shrink your stomach so you are satisfied with smaller portions of food without any feelings of hunger or deprivation.

To download the free MP3 hypnosis audio to 'Shrink your stomach' go to www.your7simplesteps.com and click on the Hypnosis tab.

Hypnosis to reduce stress

Emotional eating is often a result of feeling stressed and overwhelmed. Listen to this powerful stress-buster to support you in releasing stress without swallowing it down with food.

> *To download the MP3 'Stress buster' audio go to www.your7simplesteps. com and click on the Hypnosis tab.*

Hypnotic guided visualisation for a slimmer, healthier you

The ability to visualise yourself as slim and fit is key to helping you achieve your weight-loss goal. We would go so far as to say if you cannot visualise yourself at your goal weight, it will be almost impossible for you to achieve it. We explain the vital role visualisation plays in successful weight loss fully on page 97. This hypnosis audio harnesses the wonderful transformative power of visualisation to deeply embed the image, feelings and sensations of a slimmer, healthier you into your subconscious. Your mind will then find new and creative ways to make this your reality.

> *To download the MP3 'Guided visualisation for a slimmer, healthier you' audio go to www.your7simplesteps.com and click on the Hypnosis tab.*

Important warning: You should not listen to any of the hypnosis audio tracks whilst driving a car or operating machinery.

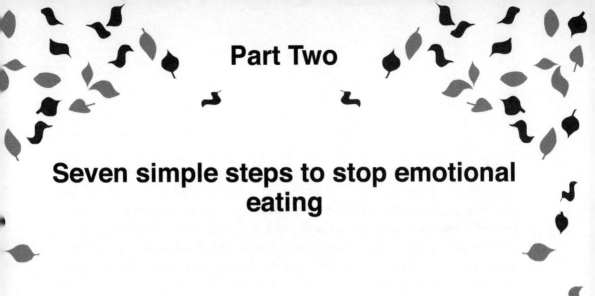

Part Two

Seven simple steps to stop emotional eating

When we work face to face with clients, in our separate practices, we generally see them for around six or seven sessions. We have structured our self-help approach along similar lines to reflect this. We have spent a great deal of time developing the steps and the order has been determined to provide the optimum outcome for you. We would really like you to begin with step one and complete it fully before moving on to the next step. Some of you may be tempted to dip in and out of the steps, or even to cherry pick, and just choose to work on the parts that appeal to you most. This ad hoc approach may mean you omit resolving emotional blocks that could stand in your way of successful weight loss. So our recommendation is to set aside an hour or so, once a week, whenever you have quiet time to dedicate to yourself, and to begin at the very beginning.

Step One: Acknowledging the present

Today is today. You are where you are now through a whole set of circumstances, and chance happenings. Some of these were within your control and many, many others were not. Acknowledge that you have only ever done the best you could do, and you already know that sometimes your best wasn't that great, but at the time that was all you could do.

Maya Angelou said, 'I did then what I knew how to do. Now that I know better, I do better.' We ask that you do the same. Allow yourself just to be, and to acknowledge where you are today without self-blame, or negative judgements. You've already come further than you think and survived times more challenging than anyone else really knows about.

The early stages of this work are designed to reveal and explore old habits and old, engrained and unquestioned ways of thinking about yourself that you may not even be fully aware of. There are revelations in this work that can surprise you. You are beginning to mine the past to recall half-remembered times which have somehow kept you stuck and influenced your relationship with food.

You are about to take a life-changing step on your road, and to see for yourself your potential to live every day as a brand new day, with a brand new dawn.

Tune in to your self-talk

We all hear self-talk – that voice in our head that can so effectively make us feel uncomfortable. Self-talk rarely talks us up or makes us feel great. It is that nagging, carping voice in our head reminding us of our limitations and our so-called failures.

We often don't even know the origin of our self-talk, but it may certainly be telling us things that we would never share with anyone else. It is there inside our mind, and most likely has been there, unexplored and limiting our self-potential, for a long, long time.

It is this negative self-talk of limiting self-beliefs and twisted half-truths about our own body and our inability to successfully lose weight, that forms the basis of our well-practised self-sabotaging behaviour. It is helpful to acknowledge this self-talk by writing it down. Shining a light onto these self-critical, self-assassinating beliefs is the first step in taking away their power.

So, what is your self-talk saying to you?

Below are some examples of self-talk from our clients. There is a worksheet on page 56 for you to use to record your own self-talk. You must first tune in to this, listen to it, and then write down what you hear. Take the time to really listen to your self-talk so you can identify whose voice or attitude it mimics. You may hear statements such as:

> *'I'm fat because I'm lazy.'*
> *'I'm overweight because I have no will power.'*
> *'I deserve to be fat.'*
> *'My body is gross.'*
> *'I can't help being big. My weight is genetic.'*
> *'I'm big boned. I'm known as big Sue/Dave [or whomever].'*
> *'I have a slow metabolism.'*
> *'I don't deserve to be slim.'*
> *'Nothing works for me.'*

Now it's your turn:

- Sit quietly.
- Tap with a soft fist on your collarbone and tune in to your self-talk.
- Don't expect your self-talk to be realistic, sensible or logical; don't judge it; just acknowledge it by writing it down. Really hearing and acknowledging your self-talk is the first step to letting it go.

- Each time you write out a sentence or phrase from your inner voice, give it a Subjective Unit of Discomfort (SUD), numbered from zero to 10. Zero equals 'I don't believe that at all' and 10 is equal to 'I believe it strongly'.
- Remember to observe whose voice, attitude, choice of words or inflection your self-talk reminds you of. The insights you discover here may also guide future work.
- The self-talk with the highest SUD number attached to it is where you begin your work. EFT or PSTEC would be excellent tools to do this.

See the 'Your self-talk' worksheet on the next page.

For the A4 printer-friendly version of the 'Your self-talk' worksheet go to www.your7simplesteps.com and click on the Worksheets tab.

Reveal your hidden limiting beliefs

Limiting beliefs are often unspoken thoughts that are never questioned. These thoughts are rarely shared or ever see the light of day, existing as they do in the shadow-lands of our conscious mind. They remain untested and taken for the truth, even though that is most often not the case.

However, what limiting beliefs do is keep you in your place. They stop you from ever even attempting your goals, or they encourage subconscious self-sabotaging behaviour to make sure you never achieve them.

Some examples of limiting beliefs that we have heard from our clients are:

'I've never been slim. It's just not possible for me.'
'Even if I lose weight I can't keep it off.'
'Everyone in my family is big. It's my genes.'
'My friends won't like me if I lose weight.'
'Everyone will expect more of me if I lose weight.'
'I'm going to have to go out and live if I lose this weight.'
'I won't feel safe being slim, healthy and gorgeous.'
'Diets have never worked for me, and this won't help either.'

Your self-talk

In the following worksheet you have the chance to bring your limiting beliefs out into the light. Acknowledging them, and perhaps noting where they originated, is a vital step in releasing beliefs that hold you back and stop you from fulfilling your full potential. Here's how you do it:

- Sit quietly.
- Tap with a soft fist on your collarbone and tune into your unspoken limiting beliefs about yourself around successful weight loss.
- Think about how other people manage their eating and their physical wellbeing. Contrast those thoughts with your beliefs about yourself.
- Take your time to really get in touch with your limiting beliefs. As in the previous worksheet, do not expect your limiting beliefs to be realistic, sensible or logical. Don't judge or edit them. Write down as many as you can. Hearing and acknowledging them is the first step to recognising them for the nonsense they truly are.
- Each time you note down one of your limiting beliefs, give it a Subjective Unit of Discomfort (SUD) number from zero to 10. Zero equals 'I don't believe that at all' and 10 is equal to 'I believe it strongly'.

To help with this, use the 'Limiting beliefs' worksheet on page 58.

To download the A4 printer-friendly PDF of the 'Limiting beliefs' worksheet go to www.your7simplesteps.com and click on the Worksheets tab.

Limiting beliefs

Eliminating your limiting beliefs

As we explain on page 39, PSTEC is a technique created to remove or break the negative emotional connection to an uncomfortable memory, or an event. We use it extensively in our work to tackle the many aspects and layers of negative emotion that encourage stress and comfort eating. The audio technique uses pre-recorded rhythmic clicks ('click tracks') to which the listener responds by following the instructions and finger tapping in time to the click tracks. The audio tracks include extensively researched, and well-accepted, psychological approaches to help make the changes you desire. The basic tracks can be downloaded free from www.your7simplesteps.com (see the Free PSTEC click tracks tab) but there are additional click tracks designed to turbo-charge your results and build on the effects of the free click tracks. These optional click tracks can be purchased for a small fee as described on our website.

The PSTEC click tracks are really designed for dealing with negative feelings in response to uncomfortable memories from the past. They are also effective with events that have only been imagined. PSTEC works wonderfully to clear limiting beliefs and old patterns of behaviour and thinking that keep you overweight and stuck.

You should begin by focusing your PSTEC work on the negative limiting belief that you scored highest on the 'Lmiting beliefs' worksheet. Here is an example of how to use the free PSTEC click tracks with the belief *'My friends won't like me if I lose weight.'* To deal with this limiting belief we recommend the following procedure, using the click tracks in the way outlined on page 41:

- Focus on the memory of not being liked by your friends while using the PSTEC free click tracks. Essentially, you want to eliminate the negative feeling of this so that it can no longer affect you or influence your behaviour.
- To do this, imagine your friends rejecting you and try to really feel the negative emotion whilst using the free PSTEC click tracks.
- Alternatively, you may have a memory of a time when you lost weight

in the past and a friend made a disparaging comment to you, or said something about your weight loss that has stayed with you. In that case, focus on that memory when working with the free PSTEC click tracks.

- If you do decide to purchase additional PSTEC tracks – for example, the optional PSTEC Positive click track (see page 186), which helps embed positive suggestions – it is still important firstly to deal with the emotional component of any beliefs by using the free click tracks first as detailed on page xx. Dealing with, and eliminating, the negative emotion helps you to change the belief.
- Remember to observe where the unhelpful belief originated. How long have you had this belief? This insight may also guide future work.

Explore your past with the timeline protocol

We have included a worksheet for you to plot your weight history from the beginning, at your birth, all the way up to today.

The focus of the Timeline protocol is to explore times in your life when your body has felt in balance, and the times you have manifested imbalance by carrying excess weight. When did this start for you? What events in your life coincided with periods of weight gain, or periods of weight loss?

The dates in themselves are not important. Focus on what you were doing at key times in your life, and how you felt then while acknowledging the effect this had on the weight you carried at those times.

Here are some examples of Timeline events from some of our clients:

'I have always been heavy; I was even a heavy toddler.'
'My mum told me I was a premature baby so I needed feeding up.'
'I was six years old, and moved mid-term from my infant school, and lost all my friends.'

Other key events that commonly play a factor in weight gain or loss are:

- uncomfortable, or confusing, sexual attention.
- traumatic experiences or events, either experienced at first-hand or witnessed.
- bullying at school, or in the work place.
- puberty and physical changes.
- parents' divorce.
- leaving home.
- feeling out of one's depth and overwhelmed.
- financial stress.
- birth of own children.
- relationship breakdown.
- redundancy.

Life events are legion. You will have your own unique history and we invite you to consider these events, perhaps for the first time, in relation to the weight you carry. Carrying excess weight can be an expression of a survival strategy formulated in times of great personal stress. Acknowledging this can be the beginning of letting go of old and entrenched patterns of behaviour that no longer serve you.

Here's how to do it:

- Go to the Timeline worksheet on page 62 or download a copy from www.your7simplesteps.com (click on the worksheets tab).
- Draw a long straight line down the centre of the worksheet with a ruler from top to bottom. One end of the line represents your birth and the other end represents today.
- Look back through your life events and write each on the worksheet. How has your body reflected pressure and change in your life so far? What family legends or stories surround your birth and early years? Consider the milestones in your life and gain an awareness of when your body felt in balance and when your body felt out of control. If during your life you have ever achieved your target weight, what happened around that time to change that for you?
- As you consider your timeline, do any events or memories still hold an emotional charge for you? The free PSTEC click tracks would be perfect

Timeline

for resolving and releasing those negative emotions so that you can no longer be triggered by them in the future.

To download the A4 printer-friendly PDF of the 'Timeline' worksheet go to www.your7simplesteps.com and click on the Worksheets tab.

Clear your resistance to change

Clearing your resistance to change is core to your work. Holding onto unwanted excess weight is often about unacknowledged fear of change. You might feel incredulous when you read that sentence, given you consciously know how much you want to lose your excess weight. However, some resistance can be very deeply buried, perhaps even below your level of conscious awareness.

So, what is behind your resistance to change? Here are some examples of resistance to change, or of fear of change, from our clients. The next worksheet (see page 64) is for you to tune in, listen and write out your own unique resistance, and fear of change. Here are some examples that may help prompt you to recognise yours.

'My friends won't like me if I lose this weight.'
'I might want more from my life if I lose this weight.'
'What happens if I lose this weight and my life is still awful?'
'It's too late for me to lose this weight. I've wasted all these years being big.'
'If I get slimmer, I might not be able to stop.'
'If I lose weight I may have to take my place in the world and be more successful, attractive, sexy...'
'I can stay safe by staying fat.'
'Being fat makes me invisible.'
'I've always been the fat one in my family.'
'I don't want them to think that I am fixed.'

Resistance to change is similar to the many layers of an onion, and it is a theme we will return to later. Being willing to take the time to peel back the

Resistance

layers and allowing your resistance to rise to the surface is important work.

Another way of considering this topic is to think about these questions:

> *'What do I maintain by staying the same?'*
> *'What possible benefits can there be for me from not changing?'*
> *'What am I saying by not losing my excess weight?'*

Initially you might think there cannot possibly be any positive gains from staying as you are, but give yourself time and space to consider this. As always with this work, it is important not to judge phrases or insights that pop into your mind. This is not about logical thinking. Just tap and breathe. Every time you allow another aspect of your old cruddy stuff to emerge you will be another step further on your way to thinking, and believing, differently about yourself.

Here is your opportunity to explore your resistance to change. Be aware you might be tempted to skip this worksheet altogether. That would be just another manifestation of resistance.

- Take your time. Breathe. Tap on your collar bone. You can close your eyes if it is appropriate to do so, and allow your mind to drift. You are going to those places in your mind so often drowned out by your busy life so give yourself time to find your quiet core. It is where, so often, the answers are.
- When you have experienced your 'Ah ha!' moments, it would be good to clear the emotions around those thoughts with PSTEC. Track back through those thoughts until you recall earlier patterns of thinking, or perhaps even the first time you had that thought. Get in touch again with what was happening for you then. PSTEC works wonderfully well on past events, both real and imagined, so play with this and do the work to clear whatever comes to mind.

> *To download the A4 printer-friendly PDF of the 'Resistance to change' worksheet, go to www.your7simplesteps.com and click on the worksheets tab.*

EFT resistance-to-change script

Emotional freedom technique (see page 21) is a powerful tool for building emotional health. It uses tapping on the 'meridians' of the face and upper body long used in Chinese medicine and now confirmed by modern western research, coupled with 'scripts' of things to say/think while following a systematic programme of tapping. The EFT resistance-to-change script is a powerful tapping script that helps tackle resistance to change no matter what form this resistance takes.

As we explain in the detailed guide to EFT (see page 22), you do not need to follow our scripts word for word. Our recommendations are a rule of thumb; it would be more powerful if you used some of the insights you have made from your own layers of resistance, so feel free to adapt or even re-write the script that follows using the EFT script template (see below).

Do have a glass of water to hand, and sip regularly.

> To download the A4 printer-friendly EFT aide memoir PDF, go to www. your7simplesteps.com and click on the EFT tab
> To download the A4 printer-friendly EFT blank template PDF go to www. your7simplesteps.com and click on the EFT tab.

EFT set-up for first tapping round

As we explain on page 22, EFT involves a number of 'rounds' of tapping the meridian points, each beginning with a 'set-up' phase. For each phase and round a different script is used. Scripts you have worded for yourself are most powerful so the following is an approximate model for you to follow and adapt. For the set-up phase of the first round we recommend, while tapping on one hand with the other, or on your 'sore sport':

> 'Even though I want to be healthy and eat nourishing foods, I don't want to do this, and you can't make me and I completely and fully love and accept myself as I am, even though it's hard for me.'

> 'Even though I don't want to do this and I do want to do this and I

can't make me do it, I completely and fully love and accept myself as I am now even though it's hard for me to accept myself.'

'Even though I don't want to be fit, lithe and healthy, I do and I don't and I will and I won't and NO, NO, NO, NO, NO – you can't make me – and I deeply and completely love and accept myself without any judgement.'

First round of tapping

Each round should only take about 30-40 seconds. The letters before each statement refer to the meridian points shown in Figure 1 on page 25:

EB:	'No! You can't make me be healthy and fit.'
SE:	'I just don't want to.'
UE:	'Yes, I do want to be healthy and fit.'
N:	'No, I don't.'
C:	'You can't make me.'
CB:	'No! No! No! No! No!'
RIBS:	'Please! Don't make me be healthy and fit.'
UA:	'I have to... I just have to...'
W:	'I can... I can't... I will... I won't... I must... I mustn't...'
TH:	'I have to... I just have to...'

Take a breath...

EFT set-up for second tapping round

As before, these are model set-up statements to use prior to the second round of tapping on the meridian points.

'Even though I am not healthy now, I choose to be healthy and I deeply and completely love and accept myself without any judgement.'

'Even though clearly I am not healthy, I choose to be healthy and I deeply and completely love and accept myself without any judgement.'

'Even though I am confused about good health, I choose to be healthy and I deeply and completely love and accept myself without any judgement.'

Second round of tapping
These are the approximate statements for each meridian point you tap in the second round:

EB: 'I say YES to health, today, right now...'
SE: 'No! I say yes to staying the way I am'
UE: 'You can't make me be fit, lithe and healthy.'
N: 'You can't make me change.'
C: 'You can't make me fat.'
CB: 'No wonder I'm confused.'
RIBS: 'You can't make me be fat and unhealthy... I choose to be in control'.
UA: 'You can't make me do anything and I now choose health and wellbeing.'
W: 'I say YES to health and wellbeing.'
TH: 'I choose health and wellbeing today.'

Take a breath...

EFT set-up for third tapping round
'Even though I've been stuck, I do want to live my dreams and I deeply and completely love and accept myself without any judgement.'

'Even though I'm not taking enough action, I intend to live my dreams and I deeply and completely love and accept myself without any judgement.'

'Even though I'm stuck and it's all my fault, I choose to live my dreams anyway and I deeply and completely love and accept myself without any judgement.'

Third round of tapping
These are the statements for each meridian point you tap in the third round:

EB: 'No, I don't, and you can't make me.'
SE: 'I want to live a fulfilling life.'
UE: 'No, I want to be miserable and lonely.'
N: 'You can't make me have joy.'
C: 'You can't stop me from living my dreams.'
CB: 'I've been so stuck.'
RIBS: 'I choose to live my dreams.'
UA: 'You can't make me stay stuck... I choose to be in control.'
TH: 'I say YES to life, love, and peace...and to being the biggest and best I can be, today, right now!'

Take a deep breath.

EFT set-up for fourth tapping round
'Even though I've been arguing with myself, I deeply and completely love and accept all of me.'

'Even though I've been saying NO to myself, I deeply and completely love and accept all of me.'

'Even though I've been focused on being in control rather than being creative and flexible, I deeply and completely love and accept all of me.'

Fourth round of tapping
These are the statements for each meridian point you tap in the fourth round:

EB: 'It's okay to say no.'
SE: 'It's okay to say yes.'
UE: 'I'm sick and tired of saying yes and no at the same time.'
N: 'I've decided to be clear.'
C: 'It's okay to be safe, and say yes.'
CB: 'It's my choice.'
RIBS: 'It's OK for me to say yes.'
UA: 'I'm in control.'
TH: 'I love feeling safe, free, and in control of what I choose for my life, today, right now.'

Take a deep breath... and another... and now, one more big one...

Now, say to yourself in your best imitation of a three-year-old:

'No! You can't make me!'

Note: Inspired by a Rick Wilkes EFT script.

Review
How does that all feel? What emotions came up as you tapped around? What memory or idea do you feel would be good to tap on next? Remember there is no right or wrong to tapping. A round of tapping takes only a few moments – so what's there to lose? If other words pop into your head as you are tapping around, simply forget the text written here and go with your own words and thoughts. The more you make this yours the more it will resonate with you and the more changes you will experience in your thinking and feeling.

Remember your words are always the most powerful so take this opportunity now to compose your own EFT script on this theme.

> To download the A4 printer-friendly EFT blank template PDF go to www. your7simplesteps.com and click on the EFT tab.

Clear resistance with PSTEC

The time you spend working through this book will help you to focus on, and appreciate, your own intuition. Perhaps you already have a growing awareness of your particular kind of resistance to change, and the part it plays in keeping you overweight and stuck? Often 'Aha!' moments, or moments of clear insight and realisation, come with increased awareness.

Perhaps you realise now that the last time you lost weight brought you too much attention from the opposite sex making you feel uncomfortable? Does your partner give you the impression that he/she prefers you just the way you are so you're afraid your relationship will be jeopardised if you change by losing weight? Will you be the only slim one in your family if you lose weight, so there's a part of you that is afraid to be successful as you may no longer be accepted? Is there a part of you that feels you kept yourself safe by being overweight, and that you may be expected to go out and socialise more when you are slim? Have you failed many times in the past, and fear that what works for other people just will not work for you, and you cannot face failing again?

Imagine the key scenario that is causing the most resistance. Use one of the free click tracks to clear the fear and anxiety, and then see how you're feeling about losing weight. If you feel comfortable and safe to lose weight, then you're done. If not, sit quietly and imagine yourself at your goal weight. What are the feelings? Is there still some resistance left? Can you work out what is causing it? If you can, then use one of the free click tracks to clear it.

If you're unable to picture yourself at your goal weight you will need to work on this as we have found it's nigh on impossible to be successful if you can't imagine your desired outcome. Try the following process. Imagine that standing between you as you are now, and you at your goal weight, is a barrier of some sort. What is this barrier made of? How high is it? Is there any emotion when you're looking at the barrier? Try to be spontaneous about this process. It's not about over-thinking. This works best if you just make a note of whatever comes into your mind. It doesn't matter if it's illogical, or absurd. Try not to judge your responses. What SUD rating is the emotion when you focus on your barrier? Now run one of the free click tracks on this. Persevere as it may take you a few rounds for the barrier to eventually disappear, leaving you able to see yourself at your goal weight. When you can (and you will), well done!

Work with the free click tracks on all your negative emotions around achieving your goal weight. You can turbo charge your results by working with one of the optional purchase tracks, called PSTEC Positive or PSTEC Positive Extra, to help embed positive suggestions into your subconscious once you have cleared your resistance.

Reset your personal hunger dial

Figure 3: Understanding and resetting your personal hunger dial
Resetting your hunger dial gives you an opportunity to pause and assess what is happening around your hunger levels, and your desire to eat. So often, compulsive eating and sugar cravings are nothing at all to do with being hungry and are driven by emotional needs. A new awareness of what is driving your hunger allows you to pause and find new and improved ways of taking care of yourself without swallowing down your emotions with unnecessary food.

Cravings and the need to avoid being hungry are closely associated. If you haven't eaten for a few hours and your stomach feels empty, and is maybe even rumbling, then this could be real hunger. The best way to check is to have a glass of water. If you're still feeling those empty feelings and rumblings in about 15 minutes, you're definitely hungry.

If you have just eaten a meal and feel that you still want more, this is simply a desire to eat rather than actual hunger.

If you have a really strong urge to eat a particular thing and you also experience feelings of tension, then this is a craving.

Remember that cravings will go away. Distract yourself. Go and get a glass of water. Get up and pat the dog. Ring a friend. Remove yourself from the situation and you'll find the craving passes. It is only a thought and thoughts can be changed! If you see a craving as life-or-death, that needs to be dealt with immediately – for example, *I really fancy that muffin and I need to have it now'* – then you can change this. Say to yourself: *'This is just a craving, which is just a thought, that's all... I don't have to take any notice of it. If I concentrate on something else for just a few minutes I'll forget all about it and I'll be really pleased with myself that I didn't eat something that I didn't really need.'*

Some deep breathing is often helpful as well. You'll feel more relaxed and the craving should have passed. If you're finding it impossible to let go of that craving though, use the click track to clear it.

Full... or satisfied?

The full feeling we experience usually comes from eating bulky carbs, particularly bread.

Try preparing a low-carb meal that looks the right size and eat it. You will find that you won't get the 'full feeling', but it will be a right-sized meal and you will feel **satisfied**. In fact, you don't want the full feeling as that would mean you've eaten too much. That full feeling is no longer wanted. In fact it's a bad feeling! The better feeling is to have eaten a small low-carb meal and not feel full and bloated... but knowing that you have eaten a healthy and satisfactory meal.

If not feeling full and bloated feels scary for you, then run the click track on that fear.

The pause button

Using the 'pause button' is a really effective technique you can use for times when you are feeling tempted to eat something that you know very well you don't need.

In cognitive behavioural therapy (CBT) the problem is called suffering from 'low frustration tolerance'. What this means is that basically you can be perfectly controlled and self-disciplined in various other areas of your life – maybe you don't drink or smoke, for example – but when you are faced with this one particular thing (in this case food), you suddenly feel completely helpless and powerless. It's as if this thing has some sort of hold over you... like it's consuming your whole being and turning you into a quivering wreck. You may even feel that the urge is so strong that if you don't go ahead and give in to it, then you will literally just about collapse in a heap and die. Does that sound familiar?

This is when the 'pause button' is helpful.

Imagine that you have a remote control for your own life (similar to the one for your TV) so you can pause/fast forward/rewind as and when necessary.

Picture yourself there – that food you really want is right in front of you (crisps... biscuits... chocolate...) – and you're starting to feel weak, wanting to gulp it down on the spot. Quick as a flash you must hit your pause button to freeze-frame yourself physically for the next few seconds. Now, while you are on pause, physically spend the next few seconds running through the whole scenario mentally in your head and seeing yourself eating whatever it is you're tempted by and enjoying (or not!) a few quick seconds of gratification from it.

Then you need to fast-forward (mentally) to five minutes AFTER you've finished eating and think about how you're feeling then and what you're thinking. This will probably be the usual routine of feeling guilty, beating yourself up, telling yourself you're stupid for eating all that unnecessary food... and so forth.

So now you've reminded yourself of exactly how bad you're going to feel if you DO go ahead and eat this, you can mentally rewind back to the present and spend a few moments playing through the scenario once more, but this time add in the nice happy ending and see yourself recognising that you're not actually hungry and you don't really need this food... it's just a craving which is no more than a thought that starts in your mind... and you are completely in control of your thoughts if you choose to be.

Consequently, you see yourself deciding to walk away from the food and then fast-forward to five minutes later. Now how are you feeling? Probably strong, positive and proud of yourself because at last you've reacted in the right way and done the right thing!

The reality is that the initial thought you had can be built up out of all proportion or stopped in its tracks. The choice is yours. You are the one in control.

Rewind mentally to the present and notice that there were two different possible outcomes to this situation – giving in to the craving and then feeling bad about it, or not giving in and then feeling good – and it's up to you to choose which path you want to take.

After all that imagining, take yourself off pause and make your choice. Same old road by eating all that unnecessary food and putting up with the negative consequences that follow? Or the positive route of not eating the food and taking a step towards achieving your target weight? The choice is yours.

Resetting your hunger levels with EFT

Here we offer an EFT (emotional freedom technique) script for resolving and releasing the desire to graze after dinner, when you are not actually hungry but still feel compelled to eat. If in fact your personal compulsions occur at a different time of day, or perhaps a different location, such as in the car or during the afternoon at the office, then you can just adapt the words to suit.

EFT set-up for first tapping round

'Even though I graze at night, I completely and fully love and accept myself.'

'Even though I don't know how to stop this grazing after dinner, I completely and fully love and accept myself as I am now.'

'Even though I graze in the evening and I don't want to stop it because I really enjoy it, I completely and fully love and accept myself without judgement.'

Firstly take three fairly deep and gentle breaths. Breathe in through your nose and softly out through your mouth. Don't use any force or pressure.

Now focus for a moment on your desire to graze on food and assess the level of desire.

First round of tapping

EB: 'I can't stop this grazing,

SE: 'and I don't think I want to anyway

UE: 'because it's a reward for me after a long tiring day.'

N: 'It's a satisfying way to end my day,

C: 'and I don't think I want to stop,

CB: 'even though my health is suffering and I'm eating far too much.'

RIBS: 'All this extra food is making me fatter and fatter,

UA: 'but I really enjoy these extra snacks,

W: 'even though I know they're no good for me,

TH: 'but I'm not sure I can let this habit go.'

Pause. Take one easy, deep breath.

EFT set-up for second tapping round

'Even though I still have this desire to graze in the evening, I completely and fully love and accept myself.'

'Even though my desire to graze in the evening feels like a habit I can't release, I completely and fully love and accept myself as I am now.'

'Even though I'm not sure I can stop this grazing in the evening, part of me wants to change and I completely and fully love and accept myself without judgement.'

Second round of tapping

EB:	'Part of me does want to change,
SE:	'even though I'll miss the comfort of that food,
UE:	'but it's such an unhealthy thing for me to do,
N:	'so I'm willing to start to let this habit go.'
C:	'Perhaps I can start to change my thinking around this grazing habit
CB:	'and see this behavior for what it is –
RIBS:	'just a way of escaping.'
UA:	'I choose to release this habit easily and effortlessly,
W:	'even though I'm afraid I'll miss the comfort of
TH:	'this habit of grazing at night.'

Pause. Take one easy, deep breath.

Assess your level of desire and rate it again from zero to 10.

EFT set-up for third tapping round

'Even though I'm still in the habit of grazing after dinner, I completely and fully love and accept myself.'

'Even though I am carrying all this stress and tension in my body and eating helps to calm it down, I completely and fully love and accept myself as I am now.'

'Even though I'm still in the habit of eating at night after dinner I choose to release and let go of this habit easily and effortlessly.'

Third round of tapping

EB: 'I'm choosing to release this grazing habit now.'

SE: 'I'm choosing to soothe myself in positive, healthy ways.'

UE: 'I'm choosing to calm all this stress and anxiety in ways that are healthy for me.'

N: 'I'm releasing this need to graze.'

C: 'I'm releasing it from every cell of my body.'

CB: 'I love this feeling of being in control.'

RIBS: 'I can easily let my thoughts go and be in control.'

UA: 'They are only thoughts and I can ignore them and choose to be in control.'

W: 'I'm choosing health and happiness now.'

TH: 'I'm choosing to change this pattern easily and effortlessly!'

Pause.

Take one easy, deep breath.

Assess your level of desire for grazing and rate it from zero to 10. You should repeat the first tapping round if required to further reduce your SUD rating.

You know when you are most likely to habitually eat even though you are not hungry, so use this opportunity to reset your hunger dial by composing your own EFT script.

> To download the A4 printer-friendly EFT blank template PDF go to www. your7simplesteps.com and click on the EFT tab.

Build your own 'dream-come-true' protocol

Building a dream-come-true (DCT) protocol is a transformational process to allow you to move your current thinking and belief system about your excess weight from where you are now to where you want to be. It uses goal setting, but in the most powerful way. It isn't just about setting an arbitrary goal and thinking that by writing it down you can achieve your dream-come-true. This protocol highlights for you all the ways you currently do not allow yourself to achieve your dream. So for the first time, you can clear all the blocks to your success.

Now is a good time to refer back to the moment you began this process of emotional change. We asked you at the outset to write down your goal weight, or dress or trouser size. Now is the time to remind yourself of the goal you noted down all that time ago. Does it inspire you when you re-read your goal? Do you need to adjust it, or represent it in another way? Perhaps you could try seeing yourself again fitting perfectly into a favourite dress, or looking wonderful in a well-cut suit you own or admire. Use visualisation techniques that resonate for you as these will be the most powerful.

Here's how to build your own protocol:

- Compose one simple statement, written in the first person and present tense, that represents your dream-come-true (DCT) around your weight. That means you write a statement about yourself as if you have achieved your weight loss goal now. Your DCT statement will read something like this:

  'I feel wonderful at my goal weight,___' [Write it out in full in your DCT statement]

  'I feel great now I am a size 10' [or whatever your goal size or weight is]

  'I love weighing 140 lb' [or whatever your goal weight is, in whatever measurement that has meaning for you.]

Now build on your intention. Really feel your emotions swell around your DCT statement and how that would feel for you. Re-read your statement. Allow yourself to feel the emotional pull and power of having that be your reality. Now is the time to add in the joy and self-pride in achieving your dream.

The next part of your DCT statement will read something like this:

> 'I am so proud of myself for reaching my goal weight.'
> 'I really enjoy taking care of myself and putting myself first.'
> 'I am so happy to count in my own life.'

Next, add in some real physical benefits from achieving your DCT that really appeal to you now that you have achieved your weight loss.

The next part of your DCT protocol will read something like this:

> 'I have so much energy, I can walk for miles.'
> 'I can dance all evening long.'
> 'I have so much energy to play with my kids/grandchildren/walk the dog.'

When you read back to yourself your three sentences you can see that you have begun to create a powerful intention that truly reflects what you want for yourself.

If you add more advantages and heartfelt expressions you can make your DCT statement even more compelling. Add in more emotional detail with regard to how it will feel when you achieve your dream. The completed DCT protocol may read something like this:

> 'I love weighing 120 lb. I feel fabulous in my size 12 jeans. I can walk for hours, and even run for a bus! Life is good and I feel so proud of myself for achieving my weight-loss goal.'

> 'I enjoy looking attractive and slim. The new slimmer and fitter me has stacks of energy. I deserve to look after myself. I love my new fit and lean body. I feel strong and supple. I'm enjoying again all the activities I used to do. I feel younger and more confident in myself.'

You can use the space on the 'Dream-come-true' worksheet (see page 82) to work out the most powerful statement for you. Experiment in building your own DCT statement. Think of yourself as moulding, or carving, your intention with words into something real and tangible – the new you.

This is only the beginning. Now you need to score your commitment and belief in your statement using the SUD ratings we have used for previous work. Zero represents *'I don't believe I can achieve this at all'* and 10 is *'I truly believe I can do this'*. When you initially set your belief score, it will most likely be quite low. Try not to be disheartened. Tap gently on your collar bone and breathe deeply and slowly. Re-read your completed DCT statement and allow your thoughts to drift to the reasons you think you cannot achieve your dream. These are your stumbling blocks to success. They may have been there a long time so give yourself time to explore this negative belief system.

We have found from our work with clients that common stumbling blocks to believing the dream-come-true statement are around self-esteem issues and fear of change. Make a note of the negative feelings your DCT statement evokes in you. This may be painful, but the negative thoughts are gifts as this is the work to be done. It is vital to clear the stumbling blocks to achieving your dream-come-true, or your subconscious mind will not let you succeed.

You can use EFT and PSTEC while focusing on your fear, or doubts around your own ability to succeed, or maybe even your belief that other people can do this but not you. As you clear your blocks to success, keep revisiting your statement.

To download the A4 printer-friendly PDF of the 'Dream-come-true' worksheet go to www.your7simplesteps.com and click on the Worksheets tab.

Clear the way for your dream-come-true with EFT and PSTEC

You can use EFT, or PSTEC, while focusing on fears or doubts around your own

Dream-come-true

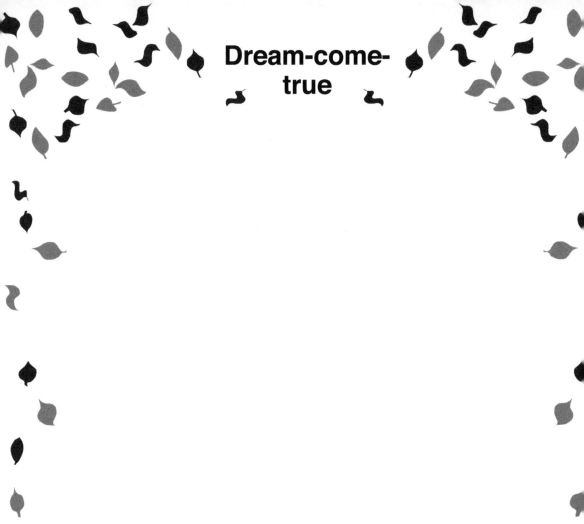

ability to achieve all the aspects of your dream-come-true statement. This may include even your belief that other people can succeed but not you.

If you want to use EFT to clear your blocks, then print out a copy of the EFT template, and using your own words compose an EFT script to acknowledge and release whatever blocks come to mind. If you compose your own EFT scripts, using your own words, the process is even more powerful and effective.

As you clear the blocks with either technique, revisit your DCT statement. You will have completed this process successfully when you score a 10 for your unassailable belief that you can embrace and achieve your DCT statement.

Affix your DCT statement to your fridge or bathroom mirror. Carry a copy with you in your wallet or handbag. Read it often. Score yourself often. If your score ever dips again then there is more clearing to be done, perhaps on an even deeper level. It is only by clearing these old blocks that you can be fully aligned with your intention.

To download the A4 printer-friendly EFT blank template PDF go to www. your7simplesteps.com and click on the EFT tab.

End your self-sabotaging behaviour around food

Sometimes we find there is an unconscious desire to remain overweight, or perhaps you have a crisis of confidence that causes you to believe it will never be possible for you to lose your excess weight. The fears do not need to be logical and these feelings and beliefs can often be at odds with your conscious efforts to lose weight.

Track back using the timeline you produced (see page 62) to when you last felt in balance with your weight or happy at the weight you were. Recall what was happening for you around this time. Was it positive or was it negative?

Think about the onion analogy again where emotions are layer upon layer and take time to unfurl to reveal deeper layers of emotion.

Find yourself a quiet, safe place. Close your eyes. Imagine yourself at your perfect, goal weight. You're looking wonderful. You're dressed impeccably. Feel all the aspects of being lighter and really enjoy your increased energy; your increased agility; the lightness of your step. Take the time to really get in touch with all of the positive emotions you can imagine yourself feeling at your goal weight. Now take yourself down a street. Just visualise yourself out walking on your own looking attractive, even sexy. People interested in you try to catch your eye. People desire you. All those years of being big and feeling invisible are stripped away and everyone can see you.

How does that feel? Does it bring up any anxieties? Use the next worksheet (see page 85) to note down any negative feelings and insecurities around being at your goal weight. If you have any negative emotions around being slim and attractive and at your goal weight then it is almost guaranteed you will never achieve it.

This is an opportunity to explore and release more aspects around resistance to change and secondary gains that keep you stuck. Your self-sabotaging behaviour may be around food, but the emotional reasons for overeating or sabotaging your weight loss will be the core of the issue so here is some space to muse and write down your insights from the guided visualisation of you at your goal weight and everything that encompasses for you.

To download the A4 printer-friendly PDF of the 'Self-sabotage' worksheet go to www.your7simplesteps.com and click on the Worksheets tab.

End self-sabotage with EFT

Self-sabotaging your own chance of success is a key theme and it crops up in our work in many different guises. We've included here two powerful EFT scripts that can assist you in releasing your own fears and doubts. Work with the one that resonates the most for you, or mix and match between the two.

Self-sabotage

EFT for self-sabotage 1

EFT set-up for the first tapping round
'Even though there's a part of me that is afraid to lose this weight, I deeply and completely love and accept myself.'

'Even though it doesn't feel safe to change, I accept myself and these feelings.'

'Even though I'm not sure who I'd be if I did lose this weight, I accept myself just as I am without judgement.'

First, take three fairly deep and gentle breaths. Breathe in through your nose and softly out through your mouth. Don't use any force or pressure. Now focus for a moment on your feelings of self-sabotage and assess how strong they are from zero to 10.

First round of tapping
EB: 'It's not safe to change.'
SE: 'I'm not sure I really want to let go of this weight.'
UE: 'Others may not like it if I let go of this weight.'
UN: 'I really hate upsetting others.'
C: 'Who will I be if I let go of this weight?'
CB: 'It's so scary to change.'
RIBS: 'I might not recognise myself.'
UA: 'I'm just going to stay fat.'
W: 'It doesn't feel safe for me to lose this weight.'
TH: 'Maybe I'll attract too much attention if I lose all this weight.'

Pause. Take a deep breath.

EFT set-up for second tapping round
'Even though I feel that I'll never lose all of this extra weight, I've failed so many times before, I deeply and completely love and accept myself.'

'Even though there is a part of me that doesn't believe I can lose this weight, there is a part of me that wants to let it go and I accept myself and all these feelings.'

'Even though I've done this to myself and I've allowed myself to get big and part of me thinks it must serve me in some way, I accept myself just as I am now and forgive myself without judgement, even though that is hard for me to do.'

Second round of tapping
EB: 'It's scary to think about being slim.'
SE: 'I just know I'll always be fat.'
UE: 'I'll never be able to lose this extra weight.'
UN: 'I think I must want to be fat; it must be helping me in some way.'
C: 'Maybe I believe that those around me feel better when I'm fat.'
CB: 'There's a part of me that thinks being fat is safe.'
RIBS: 'There is a part of me that's afraid to be slim.'
UA: 'Or maybe I'll be rejected if I lose weight and look good.'
W: 'Best to stay as I am.'
TH: 'I feel safer being fat and I'd rather be fat than feel unsafe.'

Pause. Take a breath.

EFT set-up for third round of tapping
'Even though I'm still feeling scared about losing this weight and part of me wants to sabotage the process I deeply and completely love and accept myself.'

'Even though I have always sabotaged my weightloss plans in the past I'm willing to consider that perhaps I can start to make positive and permanent changes to my eating.'

'Even though I fear failure... again... I'm starting to accept responsibility for making the changes required to move forward.'

Third round of tapping

EB: 'What if I could release these feelings around being fat?'

SE: 'What if I could change and still feel safe?'

UE: 'What if being at my ideal weight would feel great?'

UN: 'What if I could trust myself to make these changes in a safe way?'

C: 'What if I could allow this weight loss to be a positive change in my life as I do what's best for me?'

CB: 'What if I could start allowing myself to lose weight right now easily and safely?'

RIBS: 'What if I could just lose this weight and feel safe?'

UA: 'What if I could feel comfortable and trust the part of me that wants this change?'

TH: 'What if I could find it easy and effortless to make these changes and still feel safe?'

Pause. Take a deep breath.

Set-up for fourth round of tapping

'Even though it's been a long and difficult struggle and I've sabotaged my success so many times, I deeply and completely love and accept myself anyway.'

'Even though I may slide back a little from time to time, I'm choosing to see myself as being successful and I accept myself without judgement.'

'Even though I've struggled in the past, I choose now to see myself making the changes needed and celebrate all successes no matter how big or how small.'

Fourth round of tapping

EB: 'I choose to believe that I am ready to release these feelings around being fat now.'

SE: 'I choose to trust that all parts of me feel safe to allow the release of these feelings and weight now.'

UE: 'I really do want to make these changes now.'

UN: 'I choose to feel safe and protected and I trust my ability to make these positive changes.'

C: 'I have decided that I deserve to make this change and I choose to start it now.'

CB: 'I choose to believe that I am easily and effortlessly allowing myself to lose weight now.'

RIBS: 'I choose to allow myself to lose weight now.'

UA: 'I thank those parts of me for looking after me in the past.'

W: 'I trust they are changing with me in positive, healthy ways.'

TH: 'I choose to know and trust that others will be happy for me as I safely achieve my ideal body weight.'

Pause. Take a few deep breaths.

EFT for self-sabotage 2

EFT set-up for the first tapping round

'Even though I've sabotaged myself in the past, I completely and fully love and accept myself.'

'Even though I've sabotaged myself in the past and I know that I'll sabotage myself in the future, I completely and fully love and accept myself as I am now.'

'Even though I'm convinced that I'll sabotage myself, I completely and fully love and accept myself without judgement.'

Firstly, take three fairly deep and gentle breaths. Breathe in through your nose and softly out through your mouth. Don't use any force or pressure. Now focus for a moment on your feelings of self-sabotage and assess how strong they are from zero to 10.

First round of tapping

EB: 'I sabotage myself every time I try and lose weight.'

SE: 'I've sabotaged myself in the past.'

UE: 'I'll sabotage myself in the future.'

N: 'I always do it.'

C: 'I've always sabotaged myself in the past,
CB: 'and I know I'll sabotage myself in the future.'
RIBS: 'I'm the world's best at sabotaging my success.'
UA: 'I will sabotage my success.'
W: 'Any success I have, I find a way to sabotage it.'
TH: 'I'm an expert at self-sabotage.'

Pause. Take one easy, deep breath.

How to clear self-sabotage with PSTEC

Your kind of self-sabotage will be unique to you. You will have made huge strides forward in resolving your emotional eating when you have cleared all the aspects of your self-sabotage.

If you are working with PSTEC, spend some time remembering times when you did something to undermine your weight-loss goal. Try to remember as many occasions as you can. Score each memory or event using the SUD rating. Always work with the memory, either real or imagined, or events with the greatest SUD score. Use the free click tracks to clear your emotions around these memories.

Learn how to accept yourself

A great deal of your time and energy can be absorbed by thinking negatively about yourself. It may be such a well-developed habit that you are hardly aware of it. One way negative thinking manifests itself relates to the voice in your head that tells you how you are doing, and how well you are doing it. Guess what? It's rarely, if ever, positive. It simply runs on an endless loop in the semi-background of your conscious mind just reminding you to feel bad about yourself.

Learning to accept yourself and to treat yourself with kindness is challenging while the negative loop continues to play. It's important to spend some time tuning in to what your inner voice is saying. Instead of allowing it free rein, ask yourself if what it is saying is true. The combination of active listening coupled with consciously questioning what the voice says to you can be enough to interrupt the endless white noise and begin to make changes from the negative towards the positive.

The way you feel about yourself goes a long way towards how the world sees you. Begin a dialogue with yourself as if you were talking about your self-doubts with the best imagined friend in the whole world.

> What would he/she say in response to your negativity?
> Would he/she say harsh words to you, or show you compassion and acceptance of who you are?

As you continue this dialogue, ensure you allow your imaginary friend time to fully communicate with you all the praise and empathy he/she feels for you. Let these words wash over you. Remember them, and repeat them to yourself often. Practise hearing yourself speak to yourself with kindness and compassion and allow it to replace the old negative loop with a new life-enhancing positive voice.

Use the 'Accept yourself' worksheet on page 92 to write down all the things a friend would say to you to help you fully absorb them.

> *To download the printer-friendly A4 PDF of the 'Accept yourself' worksheet, go to www.your7simplesteps.com and click on the Worksheets tab.*

EFT accept yourself script

EFT can be highly effective in changing your negative inner voice to one of acceptance.

Set-up for first tapping round
'Even though I don't accept myself, I accept how I feel.'

Accept
yourself

'Even though I can't accept myself as I am now, even though I want to I accept that I feel unacceptable right now.'

'Even though I can't accept myself because I don't deserve it, I accept these feelings and I accept myself as I am right now.'

Firstly, take three fairly deep and gentle breaths. Breathe in through your nose and softly out through your mouth. Don't use any force or pressure. Now focus for a moment on your breathing and assess how unacceptable you are to yourself using the SUD ratings you have used before.

First round of tapping
EB: 'I don't accept myself as I am right now.'
SE: 'I've had a really hard time.'
UE: 'No one knows how hard it's been.'
N: 'It's been a huge struggle for me,
C: 'and I feel as though I don't deserve acceptance.'
CB: 'I don't deserve acceptance by myself and I don't deserve acceptance by others.'
RIBS: 'All I want is to be accepted,
UA: 'but I have too many faults to be accepted.'
W: 'I'm not enough and I never will be enough,
TH: 'so there are so many good reasons why I shouldn't be accepted.'

Pause. Take one easy, deep breath.

EFT set-up for second tapping round
'Even though I still can't accept myself and I just want to make myself acceptable, I accept all of my feelings anyway.'

'Even though I can't see how I could ever be acceptable to myself or others, I accept all my feelings of being unacceptable.'

'Even though I'm still feeling unacceptable and I don't know what to do, I accept myself without judgement.'

Second round of tapping

EB: 'I'm still feeling unacceptable,'

SE: 'So I'm pleasing others to make myself acceptable,

UE: 'but I feel empty inside and I'm becoming resentful.'

N: 'It's just not working for me,

C: 'and I doubt it ever will because I need to start accepting me

CB: 'so I can start changing my mind.'

RIBS: 'I'm choosing to change my mind and accept that I've done the very best I could do with the resources I had.'

UA: 'But what if I change and others don't like me any more?'

W: 'I'm not sure I could handle that.'

TH: 'I need to be accepted.'

Pause. Take one easy, deep breath. Again, assess and rate from zero to 10 how unacceptable you feel.

EFT set-up for third tapping round

'Even though I'm still not accepting myself, I completely and fully love myself and accept how I feel right now, even though that's hard for me.'

'Even though I am still not accepting all of me right now, I am choosing to change my mind and be kinder to myself.'

'Even though acceptance of myself is a struggle, I choose to start seeing myself differently, which will mean that others will start seeing me differently as well.'

Third round of tapping

EB: 'I'm still not fully accepting myself,

SE: 'but I'm choosing to start changing my mind.'

UE: 'Changing my mind and changing the way I view myself

N: 'because even though it's been so hard,

C: 'the truth is, I am still here and I haven't given up,

CB: 'and I'm acknowledging that I'm feeling a little more empowered every day,

RIBS: 'and that feels exciting as I give up the struggle and start accepting me just as I am,

UA: 'and I'm choosing to do this differently now because my past behaviours haven't worked for me,

W: 'and it feels good to start accepting myself,

TH: 'and this will lead to the results that I want and deserve!'

Pause. Take one easy, deep breath. Assess again how unacceptable you feel and rate this feeling from completely unacceptable (10) to completely acceptable (zero). Repeat the first tapping round if required to further increase your self-acceptance.

Learn how to accept yourself using PSTEC

So many of us have that negative voice in our heads. It tells us we aren't good enough. It tells us we're being judged by others. It tells us we will never succeed. It tells us we don't deserve to be slim. Or healthy. Or successful. And that voice feels very real. It isn't, of course. The reality is that voice is just a part of us judging ourselves. It's time to turn that voice off!

When that negative thought comes into your mind it needs to be challenged. Perhaps you've had a thought, 'That person is staring at me and thinking I'm fat.' As soon as you hear that negative thought you need to challenge it. Ask yourself 'Is that true? Where is the evidence?' Of course there is none as you've made it up. Just let that thought go and think about something positive.

If you find you can't release the thought, and it's creating anxiety for you, it's time to use the PSTEC click track (see page 39). Go to the experience in your mind and give it a SUD rating. Keeping the emotion as high as possible, run the click track on it. After each round, check the SUD rating. Continue using the click track until it's at zero.

Choose to change

The 'Choices Method' was developed by Dr Pat Carrington and is a powerful extension of EFT. This method allows you to change a negative reaction you may be having into a reaction you choose to have.

There are three distinct rounds of EFT required to complete the choices method.

- To begin, you need to identify the negative thought, attitude or feeling you want to change. Give this a SUD level – that is a measure from zero to 10 of how strongly you believe this negative thought, with zero being not at all and 10 the highest score.
- Now, choose an antidote to this – so, if your negative thought was 'I feel angry and upset when ___' an antidote might be, 'I choose to feel centred and calm.' You should combine these two, so, you would then say, 'Even though I feel angry and upset when ___, I choose to feel centred and calm.'
- Now, do one complete round of EFT using the negative thought as a reminder phrase. So, for example, you would tap on all the points (see page 25) saying 'I feel angry and upset when___.'
- Follow this with another complete round of tapping using only the positive as a reminder, for example, 'I choose to feel calm and centred.'
- Now, perform a third round, this time alternating the negative thought and the positive antidote. At the first tapping point say, 'I feel angry and upset when ___', and at the next tapping point say, 'I choose to feel centred and calm.' Continue tapping through all the points alternating between the negative and positive, ensuring that you finish with the positive antidote.
- Check your SUD level, and, if required, repeat this process until you have reached a zero.

Always state exactly what you want. You should use a choice, such as 'I choose to immediately feel calm, relaxed and in control.' So your wording might be 'Even though I feel angry and upset when ___, I choose to immediately feel calm, relaxed and in control.'

State your choices in the positive. Avoid words and phrases such as 'no', 'don't' or 'not'. An incorrectly worded Choices Method would be 'I choose to not be anxious.' This should be worded as 'I choose to immediately feel calm and relaxed.'

Visualisation – the secret tool for successful weight loss

Over two hundred years ago the English poet, and painter William Blake said, 'Man's conceptions are limited by his perceptions; man cannot conceive that which he cannot perceive.'

In simple terms, Blake knew all that time ago exactly what so many sports heroes and successful business people today know for certain – if you can't imagine yourself, or see yourself succeeding, winning, or achieving your goal, then it will not happen – it simply can't.

So, right on cue, this is where visualising your goal of weight-loss success – and yourself actually at your goal weight – comes in.

Your subconscious mind does not know the difference between reality and imagination: research with top athletes has shown that the improvement achieved by those who merely sat and imagined shooting the ball on the basketball court was equal to those who physically practised every day![10]

The brain works best with visual stimuli. A picture of yourself when you were happy with your weight, your life and everything that was going well for you would be an ideal visualisation to focus on for a moment or two before you sleep so that your brain knows very clearly what it is you desire. If such a picture does not exist for you, or becomes complicated with other feelings, then simply find a picture in a magazine of the physical size and shape you are aiming for and focus on that instead.

A visualisation aid can be as simple as a single picture. However, a scrap book of several images makes the whole process more powerful and evocative and reinforces your goal within your subconscious mind. You can include pictures of clothes that you want to wear; exotic beaches you want to run along; pictures of ideal partners you want to be with; even your dream house. You can add sensual fabric scraps as well that appeal to you – they could be leather, lace or silk – it's your choice. Give your brain the visual stimulus it needs to clearly know the goals you have in mind.

And add notes too. Make them present tense, in the here and now, and not set in the future or that is where your goals will stay – some time ahead of you, just out of arm's reach.

Now add the emotions. Your subconscious wants to know what you'll be feeling when you've achieved your goal, so put these emotions into the mix as well. Allow yourself to feel the pride you are experiencing as you imagine someone commenting on how awesome you look now that you have reached your goal weight. Allow yourself to feel the excitement as you imagine trying on that gorgeous dress or suit designed for someone slim... the absolute delight you feel as you imagine buttoning up your shirt without that big stomach nearly popping all the buttons... how wonderful it feels after you have easily walked up to the top of that steep hill on your holiday where the view is amazing. Really feel those emotions and intensify them as much as you can.

Release any feelings of desperation you may be experiencing because you will only attract more of those otherwise. Take yourself to a lovely relaxed place and feel yourself having achieved your goal easily and effortlessly. If the desperate or negative feelings persist, then use EFT or PSTEC to let them go.

Stay with the visualisation for at least two minutes. Repeat this during the day as often as you can – the more often you do it the better the results will be. Make it the last thing you do at night as you settle down to sleep. Feel it just as though you have it all now.

Mental imagery is very powerful, especially when used in conjunction with hypnosis. The mind is capable of using imagery to assist us in creating what we desire. Listen to one of the hypnotherapy audio tracks (see page 186) on a daily basis to keep up the positive reinforcement and suggestions that work on a very deep level with your subconscious mind.

As mentioned earlier, the subconscious cannot tell the difference between reality and imagination so picture or imagine yourself having achieved your ideal weight and feeling content eating small portions, for example. Your mind will then believe that it must create that scenario and work with you as you move towards your goal. As long as you are highly motivated to achieve your natural weight and have dealt with all your resistance, fears and old self-sabotaging behaviours with EFT or PSTEC, then it will happen just as you visualise it.

Visualisation – using the technique

Here is a great visualisation technique to help get your subconscious mind on board with your weight loss.

- Sit in a quiet place where you won't be disturbed.
- Hold out your left hand and imagine you are putting into the palm of this hand an image of yourself as you are now. Make this image a grey or sepia colour.
- Now, hold out your right hand and in the palm put an image of yourself at your ideal weight. Notice the gorgeous clothes you're wearing... see how confident you're feeling... feel the shape of your slim, trim and healthy body. Make this image bright and intense.
- Now, take that image in your left hand and allow it to shrink until it's the size of a tiny grain of sand. Blow that grain of sand away into the wind.
- Look at the image in your right hand again and now make it even brighter and more intense. Keep increasing the brightness until you are looking absolutely radiant and fantastic. Then allow yourself to feel the emotions you are experiencing... pride, confidence, healthy etc. Feel those emotions in every cell of your body and keep intensifying them until they just can't get any stronger.
- Now bring your right hand over to your left hand and put your palms together. Bring both your palms to your chest and allow this image into your body. Feel it permeating every nerve, muscle, fibre and tissue of your body.

- Breathe in deeply and be that new you. Take a minute or two and allow that image to really settle inside of you.

This exercise can also be done in your mind and therefore virtually anywhere. If you have a few minutes sitting on a bus, train or tram, just close your eyes and do it. The more often you do this, the more you will be reinforcing your desires in your subconscious mind.

To download Guided visualisation mp3 go to www.your7simplesteps.com and click on Hypnosis Resources.

Emel's story

Emel's story was given in an interview with Sally and is included here with Emel's permission.

'The journey to the seaside was exciting and I remember being really happy. Everything changed when he took me into the bushes and did what he wanted to do to me. Everything was hot and bright. He then carried me into the sea. I remember the waves crashing over my head and me losing my footing. I was tiny; there was nothing of me. I was five, maybe six years old. The waves were big, but he was insistent and pulled me into the surf anyway.

'The sexual abuse began that day, with the sea's breakers washing away what he had done to me. It was confusing and alarming. He was my Dad. I loved my Dad but he hurt me and told me to keep quiet and this secret thing of his kept happening to me whenever he managed to get me on my own.

'I was thinking about that memory today as I sat in my car outside your house. I was early and just sitting there waiting until it was time to knock on your door. So much has happened since then, and sitting waiting to see you, I really got a sense of how far I have come.'

Emel paused. 'I very nearly just said it's been one hell of a journey, but in truth it's been an amazing journey of healing and it began here, at your door all those years ago.'

Emel had come at my invitation to recall some of the work she had done with Liz Hogon and me in our early workshops. Now 70 years old, she is sprightly, slim and full of life, almost unrecognisable from the woman we first got to know.

At the time I was practising as a massage therapist specialising in working with women survivors of abuse. Emel had written to me explaining that she was interested in receiving a massage, but wanted to know exactly what that entailed before she booked an appointment. I can't remember exactly my reply, but I must have allayed her fears as the following week she booked her first appointment. I was already trained in EFT (Emotional Freedom Technique) and found it to be the perfect, natural complement to body work as a way of releasing and resolving the often profound emotional responses that physical touch can release.

Completing my intake form, Emel spoke quietly to explain that she had rarely ever been touched with kindness and she was desperate to know how that might feel to her. She said that growing up she had only known her father's sexual abuse and her mother's violent jealous rages, and savage beatings. The only real kindness she had known was the rare times with her grandmother. One time in particular she remembered resting her head against her grandmother's knee and having her hair gently stroked.

Her arranged marriage at the age of 17, to an older man she barely knew, brought her three daughters she adores to this day, but no respite from cruelty and abuse.

By the time we met she was making tentative steps towards recovery and finding herself following a mental breakdown. She had spent great swathes of her unhappy married life on anti-depressants and submitted herself to much of what was offered through the NHS (UK National Health Service) mental health services. With her daughters grown, she had finally divorced her abusive husband and was, for the first time in her adult life, living alone in her ex-marital home. Even with her survivor's spirit, her collected memories and experiences of sexual and physical violence had taken their toll on her. She was depressed, and her petite frame was over-burdened with excess weight, leaving her with stiff and aching joints. Her years of yo-yo dieting were regularly sabotaged by her compulsive cravings for sweet treats as her main source of self-comfort. Fifty-something years later, cooking dinner for herself in her own kitchen, she would habitually pick and graze from food in her cupboards, even though she knew her dinner was almost ready.

'From the age of nine I was cooking meals for my younger siblings and even as I prepared the food, stirred the pot and served it I knew there wasn't enough for me. There was never enough for all of us and that feeling of knowing I was going to go hungry was still triggering me all these years later to overeat, even when I knew good food was plentiful in my house.'

Emel described having many vivid memories of being hungry as a child. She would sometimes steal a spoonful of home-made jam from a jar in her mother's pantry. She was careful not to get caught as her mother would certainly have beaten her. Equally, her mother, in a jealous rage, would often beat her over the special attention her father paid her. In her adult life, Emel would often feel restless and uneasy after dinner, and experience the same childhood compulsion for eating something sweet.

'I would sit in the evening knowing that I had eaten my dinner. Eaten my pudding. I would know that I wasn't hungry, but I would still need something nice. Something for me, and the only way I knew to have something nice for me was to eat something sweet.'

For years Emel slept fitfully and she would often wake with a start, feeling echoes of old anxieties and fears.

'Often I would wake in the middle of the night with a panic attack and feel all those old anxieties, over and over again, and the only way I knew how to calm myself was again to eat something sweet. I can remember going down to my kitchen on many, many occasions and just stuffing food down my throat, stifling my rising fear, swallowing it down.'

Emel said that having that first massage was a powerful step for her healing.

'To allow myself to accept those good feelings in me, from being stroked and touched with kindness, was such a breakthrough for me. I began to realise I had thought it was normal to feel tense all the time, but through massage I also began to notice what feeling relaxed felt like, and I learnt to tell the difference.'

Emel had never been able successfully to lose weight following conventional diets, and she had struggled with her weight for years. She joined one of our first seven-week group workshops in London that focused on resolving and releasing the emotional connections to comfort and stress overeating.

She recalled, 'My overeating and desire for sweet things was all to do with my childhood. The only way I knew how to cope with all of the memories of cruelty and trauma I experienced with my Mum and Dad was to eat. It's all I knew.

'Working with Liz and Sally I realised how much I blamed and punished myself for what had happened to me. I believed it was somehow all my fault and if I'd been a better daughter then none of those terrible things would have happened to me. The gradual process of forgiving myself, and learning to love and cherish myself, was a life-saver for me and in turn, in time, I was able to forgive my parents. It didn't all happen at once, but for the first time I had the therapy tools and trusted my intuition enough to see things differently. From the work I did I changed how I thought about myself and the beliefs I had about me. It was never, ever my fault.'

She continued, 'The irony is that years and years later, when my Dad was an old man, I became his carer as he grew more frail and slipped into dementia, with his eventual death just a few years ago. It was a difficult time. I had so much anger towards the man who had betrayed me as a little girl and yet here was a broken, old man in front of me. I did lots of tapping (EFT). Hours of tapping!' She laughed. 'I could let it go. It's over. I've learnt to protect that little girl inside of me. She's safe with me. You and Liz showed me how to do that.'

'And,' she continued, 'there were even moments of healing with him. I remember him being very sharp and unfair with me one day when I was caring for him. Without even raising my voice I told him that I remembered everything he'd ever done to me. It stopped him in his tracks. He was about to shout at me to shut me up, but this time I stared him out. I just looked deep into his eyes. He knew. His mouth closed and he held his head in his hands in shame as he walked away from me.'

Emel continued, 'It's not as though I'm completely fixed,' she smiled, 'I thought I was. I've been very happy – much happier than ever before for many years now – but sometimes, something comes out of the blue, and I'm thrown off my feet again. When Jimmy Savile hit the news [for readers outside the UK, the investigation of a high-profile paedophile who had gone unchallenged for years], I could feel all the anger choking up in me again and I was right back there, but this time, instead of swallowing those feelings down with food, I had the therapy techniques I had learnt, and the trust in myself to understand that it's just another layer that I need to clear. I can do that.'

Having enjoyed sound sleep for a long time, Emel told me she had begun waking again in the middle of the night, feeling again traces of that old panic. 'I know what it's about though, now. Back then I never knew. I'm excited. I'm actually in the middle of selling the house I lived in with my ex-husband. I've got a buyer and everything is going through. It's the next stage of my life. Those last memories of him will go with the old house. I'm buying a bungalow and I'm staying with one of my daughters while I have it completely renovated. I want everything new and fresh because I deserve it.'

Rising to leave I commented on how well Emel looked. I asked what weight she had been when she started her work with us.

'Probably about 12½ stone, or maybe even more (81 kg/177 lb) and now I'm 9½ stone (60 kg/133 lb) and have been for a long time.

'But you know,' she smiled, 'for me it was never really about the food. It was those old, terrible memories and all of that self-hatred I had. But it's truly gone now. I'm a member of a theatre group. I sing; I act; I live well.' She paused. 'You know, I took swimming lessons and I did learn to swim. I still don't like the deep end where my feet can't feel the bottom. I get scared and tense when I'm out of my depth. I always need to be by the side so that I can hold on. It's the little girl in me, from all those years ago that he was bouncing up and down in the sea, and her little feet couldn't touch the sand. I must have passed out because I don't have any other memories of that day other than being back at home much later and my grandmother calling to me to wake me up.'

She looked off into the distance, remembering. 'Maybe that's something I need to do to help heal that little girl who was so scared that day in the sea.' Pausing again as she thought back to that day she said, 'Yes, maybe I'll do just that. Swim to the deep end. Why not?'

Emel added, 'I want my name to be mentioned. I have nothing to be ashamed of. This is his shame, not my shame. I had to learn to love myself instead of punishing and comforting myself with food.'

Authors' note on Emel's case history

Working with Emel it was clear that there were many traumatic experiences and memories to resolve and release. If each memory, or event, had been taken one at a time, it would have felt overwhelming to resolve years and years of trauma. Consequently, the way we worked with her was to encourage her to note down as many memories as possible, and to write them down as a stream-of-consciousness list with as little deliberation as possible. We worked with her using EFT while she compiled the list to reduce the distress of recalling events and memories.

Many individual events were grouped together. For instance, some were called 'The morning memories', or the 'Alone with Dad memories', or 'Mum's cruelty around food' memories. Once as many events as possible had been recalled, we asked Emel to give each memory, or group of memories, a SUD rating from zero to 10. The highest number represents the greatest level of distress connected to a memory.

We always begin focusing our work on events or memories with the highest level of distress. The analogy is when cutting down the biggest tree in the forest many other smaller trees are also knocked down at the same time. We worked through the list with Emel using EFT and PSTEC until the distress around the memory had gone and the SUD rating was reduced to zero. When returning to the list we always focused on the remaining events or memories with the highest SUD score. It only took a few rounds of EFT, and three or four repeats of the free PSTEC click tracks, to bring the highest SUD rated memories down to more manageable levels and not very long at all until they were down to zero. Checking back with the initial list, Emel confirmed that she felt very little negative emotion attached to the rest of the list. We did a couple more rounds of PSTEC to be absolutely sure those events no longer held any emotional pain for her, and then that part of our work was completed, leaving Emel feeling lighter in spirit than she ever had.

Emel's story is certainly one of the more distressing life experiences we have worked with. However, it is not uncommon for women who have suffered from uncomfortable experiences around sex, through to sexual abuse, to have this reflected in their relationship with food.

Working with your own issues of trauma, it is important at all times to keep yourself safe and only to tackle issues which you are confident will be manageable. If you are thinking of compiling your own list of negative memories or events, it may be advisable to begin your work with EFT and PSTEC at the lower end of the SUD score and work up the SUD scale as you become more experienced in working with the therapy tools. The alternative is also to seek out a therapist who can support you as you do this work.

Step Two: Comfort and stress eating

End sugar cravings and eating compulsions

You already know that you are prone to using food to comfort yourself, and that you often eat as a way of dealing with stressful situations. This is your opportunity to track back through time, and find early, or the earliest, instance of turning to food in this way. By exploring those early triggers you can release, and resolve, your compulsions to eat, and begin to find new ways of soothing yourself that do not involve eating.

Begin by considering the current events and situations that trigger you to comfort and stress eat. Focus on the feelings you experience at these times. Really get in touch with those feelings and emotions as strongly as you can, then use them as a link to track back those familiar feelings to much earlier events.

Refer to the Timeline protocol you worked with earlier in the book (see page 62). It could help you track back your familiar feelings through the years around comfort and stress eating. The Timeline worksheet enabled you to chart periods in your life when your weight felt in balance, and other times when you experienced weight gain and felt out of balance.

Allow your mind to drift back through those broad brushstrokes of time to focus not on events, but on those feelings that are familiar. Allow memories of those times to return to you, and focus on your emotional responses to whatever was happening to you. Give yourself time to feel those familiar feelings all the way back through time when you were triggered to eat in the past. Gain an awareness of what emotions you were stuffing down with food.

As you recall your emotions around these different events, on your timeline make a note on the comfort eating worksheet (see page 108) of the ones that still have an emotional heat to them. Give each one a SUD score with zero signifying no emotional heat and 10 signifying the greatest. It is very important to resolve those feelings with PSTEC and EFT.

Comfort
eating

To download the A4 printer-friendly PDF version of the 'Comfort eating' worksheet go to www.your7simplesteps.com and click on the Worksheets tab.

End comfort eating EFT script

The following script is a guide to using EFT (as described at the start of the book – page 21) to end comfort eating. As we've said before, the actual words used are purely illustrative – the most powerful words are those you come up with yourself provided they reflect the positive and negative sequences set out here.

EFT set-up for first tapping round

'Even though I need to comfort myself with food and I'm unable to stop, I completely and fully love and accept myself.'

'Even though food is my comfort because I feel loved and warm when I'm eating, I completely and fully love and accept myself as I am now.'

'Even though I use food to comfort myself when I'm stressed or feeling lost, I completely and fully love and accept myself without judgement.'

Firstly, take three fairly deep and gentle breaths. Breathe in through your nose and softly out through your mouth. Don't use any force or pressure.

First round of tapping

EB:	'I need that food so I can feel comforted.'
SE:	'Part of me is longing for that comfort
UE:	'of a full stomach.'
N:	'I'm feeling so hungry,
C:	'so hungry for love.'
CB:	'I'm drowning in stress
RIBS:	'and don't know how to feel okay.'
UA:	'I want to let these cares and woes slide right off me.'

W: 'I need that food so I can feel some relief.'
TH: 'I'm feeling scared and overwhelmed.'

Pause. Take one easy, deep breath.

EFT set-up for second tapping round

'Even though I still have this need to comfort myself with food, I completely and fully love and accept myself.'

'Even though I'm using food to make myself feel better, even though it's so bad for me, I completely and fully love and accept myself as I am now.'

'Even though I'm trying to make myself feel okay by overeating, I'm willing to see that there may be better ways to deal with these emotions and I completely and fully love and accept myself without judgement.'

Second round of tapping

EB: 'I'm trying to wipe all these emotions away.'
SE: 'I don't have the support I'm longing for, so I'm using food to soothe myself.'
UE: 'I'm trying to create the illusion of feeling full, and complete,
N: 'but the truth is it's not working very well for me.'
C: 'It's only creating more and more pain as I get fatter and fatter.'
CB: 'What if I could start being more responsible and recognising that I can support myself on an empty stomach?'
RIBS: 'Rather than just punishing my body with too much food,
UA: 'I could choose to start making some changes now,
W: 'even though it feels really scary.'
TH: 'I can start to support myself now in positive and healthy ways.'

Pause. Take one easy, deep breath. Assess your level of needing to comfort yourself with food and rate it again from zero to 10.

EFT set-up for third tapping round

'Even though I'm still scared of letting go of this need to comfort myself with food, I completely and fully love and accept myself.'

'Even though I am unsure if I can make the changes needed to move forward and be more responsible, I completely and fully love and accept myself as I am now.'

'I want to release this habit of comforting myself with food and stop this self-sabotage, so I'm now starting to find healthy and positive ways of rewarding and comforting myself.'

Third round of tapping

EB: 'I now choose to forgive myself for all the damage I've done to my body.'

SE: 'I'm choosing to find healthy and rewarding ways of soothing myself.'

UE: 'I'm releasing this old, damaging need to comfort myself with food.'

N: 'I was doing the best I could with the resources I had,

C: 'but I can see now there are better ways of taking care of myself.'

CB: 'I now know how to treat my body with love and kindness.'

RIBS: 'I'm so much stronger and more capable than I ever allowed myself to believe.'

UA: 'I love this feeling of strength and joy,

W: 'as I release all the old hurts and resentments from every cell of my body.'

TH: 'I'm feeling so powerful as I make these wonderful changes.'

Pause. Take one easy, deep breath.

Assess your level of need to comfort yourself with food and rate it from zero to 10.

Repeat the first tapping round if required to further reduce your SUD rating.

End sugar cravings and eating compulsions with EFT

If possible, before you begin working with EFT on your cravings, it is helpful to have some of your chosen craving food to hand. Choose the one that you really love best of all. If you are finding it hard to choose, then form a mental image of your favourite craving foods and score each one individually. Work with the food with the highest desirability score.

- Begin the process with the food still in its wrapper.
- Turn your phone off and go to a nice quiet place where you won't be disturbed.
- Now sit and contemplate this food. If you couldn't get hold of any then don't worry – just imagine it as clearly as you can in your mind. Looking at an image on the computer can also work very well. The key to making the changes you want is to really allow yourself to feel the desire for it. Get your desire up as high as you possibly can by imagining how delicious it's going to taste; remember how it tastes on your tongue, how it's going to make you feel inside as you eat it.
- Now determine, on a scale from zero to 10, how high is your craving desire. Zero is no desire at all and 10 is the highest possible craving. You are now ready to begin.

EFT set-up for first tapping round

'Even though I need this food [name it specifically here], I completely and fully love and accept myself.'

'Even though I'm craving this food, I completely and fully love and accept myself as I am now and I accept these feelings.'

'Even though I really want this food, I completely and fully love and accept myself without judgement.'

Then take three fairly deep and gentle breaths. Breathe in through your nose and softly out through your mouth. Do not use any force or pressure.

Now focus for a moment on your breathing and assess the level of your craving again. The number may have increased, decreased or stayed the same.

First round of tapping

EB: 'I really want it.'
SE: 'I have to have this food right now.'
UE: 'It tastes so good.'
N: 'This intense craving –
C: 'it feels overwhelming in my body.'
CB: 'My head is full of this craving.'
RIBS: 'I have to have it now.'
UA: 'I can't think of anything else.'
W: 'This craving –
TH: 'I have to have this food right now.'

Pause. Take one easy, deep breath.

EFT set-up for second tapping round

'Even though a part of me still wants this [name it specifically here], I completely and fully love and accept myself.'

'Even though there's a part of me that still wants [name it specifically here], there's another part of me, a bigger part of me, that is ready to let it go, and I completely and fully love and accept myself as I am now.'

'Even though I still want this [name it specifically here], I am now starting to choose health and wellbeing and I completely and fully love and accept myself without judgement.'

Second round of tapping

EB: 'This remaining craving,
SE: 'I just want to let it go.'
UE: 'I want better health.'
N: 'Oh no, I don't!'
C: 'Oh yes, I do!'

CB: 'I want to be healthier so I'm starting to let go of this craving.'
RIBS: 'This remaining craving –
UA: 'I'm feeling calmer now.'
W: 'I'm feeling a little more in control.'
TH: 'I'm releasing this remaining craving.'

Pause. Take one easy, deep breath.

Assess your level of craving and rate it again from zero to 10.

EFT set-up for third tapping round

'Even though I'm still craving this [name it here specifically], I completely and fully love and accept myself.'

'Even though I still have a little remaining craving, I completely and fully love and accept myself as I am now and I love and accept these feelings.'

'Even though I have a little craving still remaining, I choose to let it go effortlessly and easily.'

Third round of tapping

EB: 'This remaining craving –
SE: 'I choose to let it go easily and effortlessly.'
UE: 'I'm feeling calmer now.'
N: 'I'm feeling centred now.'
C: 'I'm feeling in control of this food.'
CB: 'I'm feeling more peaceful and in control.'
RIBS: 'I can say yes, or I can say no, to this food.'
UA: 'I'm choosing now to say no to this food.'
W: 'I'm breathing out this remaining craving.'
TH: 'I'm letting go of it easily and effortlessly.'

Pause. Take one easy, deep breath.

Assess your level of craving and rate it from zero to 10. Repeat the first tapping round if required to further reduce your SUD rating.

If you are finding it challenging to reduce your desire for this food completely down to zero, go to the EFT 9 Gamut point instructions (see page 34) and focus again on your food craving to help fully resolve this work.

To view a video sequence using EFT to release and resolve a popular food craving, go to www.your7simplesteps.com and click on the video sequences tab.

End sugar cravings with PSTEC

The click tracks are wonderfully successful in reducing and collapsing cravings.

Working with them removes the emotional pull that cravings can exert over you, leaving you feeling peaceful whenever you think about that particular food item (rather than your wanting to inhale an entire block of chocolate or packet of biscuits, for example, each time you see or think about it).

If possible, before you begin working with the click tracks on your cravings, it is can be helpful to purchase some of your craving food – the one that you really love best of all.

- Begin the process with the food still in its wrapper.
- Turn your phone off and go to a nice quiet place where you won't be disturbed.
- Now sit and contemplate this food. If you couldn't get hold of any then don't worry – just imagine it as clearly as you can in your mind. The effect should be the same. Really allow yourself to feel your desire for it. Get that desire up as high as you possibly can by imagining how delicious it's going to taste... the taste on your tongue... how it's going to make you feel inside as you eat it.
- On a scale from zero to 10, rate how high your craving is. Zero is no desire at all and 10 is the highest possible craving.
- Run the click track following the instructions. Do be aware that on the audio track, Tim Phizackerley, the creator of PSTEC, talks about negative

feelings whereas you may be feeling as though your desire for this food is something very positive. However, the reality is your over-consumption of this food is *not positive at all, and this is the focus of your work*.

So, you've done a round of the click track. Now, on a scale from zero to 10, how high is your craving for the food? Zero is no desire at all and 10 is the highest possible craving. Has the number come down? Is it the same?

If it's the same, just run the track through again. It should start coming down in intensity with the second round. Do ensure that you don't switch to another food or drink at any time when running the click track – just stay focused on the item you began with. This process works best when you just concentrate on one food or drink at a time.

If your craving has reduced, then make a note of your new number. Run the audio track again and continue to do this until you have reached a zero.

Now open or unwrap the food you were focusing on. Hold it... smell it... what happens to your level of craving now? You may find you have no desire whatsoever. If this is the case, then go ahead and have a small taste. What's that like? Does your craving go back up again or is it still at zero? If it's still at zero then you're done!

If your craving level has increased, then run the click track again, this time concentrating on the taste aspect. Continue until you get your craving down to a zero.

Clear mealtime memories with PSTEC

Not all families are happy families and not all families are emotionally healthy. Growing up as a child in a dysfunctional household can be a fraught and stressful experience, a veritable minefield to tiptoe through on a daily basis. Parents who struggle to cope; have money worries, mental health issues, drug and alcohol dependency, and crushing unhappiness, can make the landscape of childhood seem harsh and brutal.

Mealtimes will often be the arena where all the deficiencies and pressures on the household come into sharp relief. Do you have unhappy childhood memories about mealtimes in your household? Were mealtimes chaotic? Do you have memories of food being scarce, of there not being enough of it to go around so that you were left hungry? Did you witness arguments at mealtimes? Were they times of open hostility or oppressive stress?

If you have unhappy memories particularly associated with mealtimes, then write them down in your notebook. Give each one a SUD rating. Always begin working on the memory with the highest intensity, and clear it using the free PSTEC click tracks (see page 186). Use the SUD rating to check back, and when you are certain that the memory no longer has any emotional intensity, then focus on the next memory on your list. Work through your mealtime memories clearing the emotional intensity of each one with the free PSTEC click tracks.

Portion size reduction with PSTEC

If eating large portion sizes is a problem for you, then you can use the click track to deal with this.

- Turn your phone off and go to a quiet place where you will not be disturbed.
- Imagine a full plate of your favourite food in front of you. Now, on a scale from zero to 10, how high is your need to eat all of the food on your plate? Zero is no desire at all and 10 is the highest possible desire. Write this number down in your notebook.
- Run the click track following all of the instructions. Do be aware that on the track Tim talks about negative feelings whereas you may feel as though your desire to eat large portions is something very positive. However, the reality is that your large portions of food and your necessity to eat all the food on your plate are *not positive at all, and this is the focus of your work.*

After running the click track through, on a scale from zero to 10, how high is your need to eat all of this food? Zero is no desire at all and 10 is the highest possible need to finish your plate. Has the number come down? Is it the same? People often find that the image of a large plate of food starts to shrink down in size and, in some cases, even disappears.

If your number remains the same just run the track through again. The desire should start coming down in intensity with the second round of the click track.

If your desire for the large portion of food has reduced, then make a note of your new number. Run the track again and continue to do this until you have reached a point where you can't imagine eating that much food in one sitting.

When you are working with the free PSTEC click tracks to reduce your portion sizes, you may become aware that there is a part of you that is reluctant to stop eating before your plate is completely clean. This is simply another aspect of the same issue. You may need to resolve and release early parental rules on leaving food on your plate before you can successfully reduce your portion sizes. Full guidance on how to achieve this is outlined next.

PSTEC and leaving food on your plate

Many of us can recall growing up at a time when wasting food was seen as an almost criminal act. Or perhaps we were raised by adults who had grown up themselves experiencing great economic hardship. Those parents who grew up experiencing food scarcity themselves often sent a clear message to their offspring that wasting food was unacceptable.

If you have a belief system that says you must eat everything on your plate and that you will not allow yourself to scrape leftovers into the kitchen bin, then that waste will surely end up on your waist. If you feel compelled to clear your plate, you will never reach your healthy target weight.

If possible, use the leftovers for another meal, but if that's not an option you can use the click track to clear the uncomfortable emotions around your reluctance to dispose of excess food.

- Turn your phone off and go to a quiet place where you will not be disturbed.

- Imagine a plate of your favourite food in front of you. You have stopped eating before your plate is empty because you are no longer hungry. Now, on a scale from zero to 10, how high is your anxiety about throwing away the food left on your plate? Zero is no anxiety at all and 10 is the highest possible. Write this number down in your notebook.
- Run the click track following the instructions.
- Now, on a scale from zero to 10, how high is your anxiety? Zero is no anxiety at all and 10 is the highest possible. Has the number come down? Is it the same?
- If it's the same just run the track through again. It should start coming down in intensity with the second round of the click track.
- If your anxiety has reduced, then make a note of your new number. Run the track again and continue to do this until you have reached a point where you feel totally comfortable about disposing of any food left on your plate that you don't need.

Your eating secrets revealed

Some people are confused and amazed about their excess weight as they are barely aware of how often they eat, or even what they eat. Increasingly, people eat as a secondary activity while walking, driving, watching television or surfing the net, so that their food consumption barely registers with them.

It has been proven that keeping a food diary can be a useful tool to help encourage a greater awareness, and even an enhanced sense of accountability. For some people, knowing they have decided to log everything they eat makes them less likely to binge or make poor food choices.

A food diary can be even more illuminating when it makes the connection between your hunger levels, and when you actually eat. Using a zero to 10 scale, where zero is not hungry at all and 10 is ravenously hungry, you will soon be able to see a pattern in your eating. You may be surprised that you are accustomed to grazing on food most of the day, and only ever reach low levels of hunger. For some people even a slight feeling of hunger can trigger strong emotions so they eat often, with only small gaps between meals.

See below to download the Food and mood diary template and start keeping a food diary; then play detective with the evidence you compile. What are you missing or what would you rather have in your life that could be triggering you to eat?

Alternatively, you may see from your food diary that long stretches of time go by when you do not eat at all, so that by the time you do you are ravenous and feel completely out of control around food, leading to overeating or making poor food choices.

Here are some examples of trigger times from other clients. There is space on the next page to note down your own patterns of emotional eating.

- 'After dinner I feel panicked knowing there is no more food until tomorrow.'
- 'The children are in bed and I am alone downstairs with my crisps and soda.'
- 'When I drink, all my good intentions around food just go.'
- 'In the car after work I am so angry I eat biscuits the whole way home.'
- 'I park the car around the corner and eat ice-cream because he thinks I'm dieting.'
- 'I go without food all day, and eat in front of the TV all evening.'
- 'I buy my treats from different shops so the shopkeepers don't know how much I buy.'
- 'I take a tray of my favourite things to eat with me to bed – it's my comfort.'

As you complete the next page, sit quietly. Tap with a soft fist on your collarbone and tune in to your inner detective. What would your patterns of eating be telling you if you were to listen?

To download the A4 printer-friendly PDF of the 'Food and mood diary' go to www.your7simplesteps.com and click on the Worksheets tab.

To download the A4 printer-friendly 'Secrets Revealed' worksheet go to www.your7simplesteps.com and click on the Worksheets tab.

Secrets
revealed

Eat mindfully to release the habits that make you fat

As we highlighted in the previous section, 'Your eating secrets revealed', some people are eating a large percentage of their food intake while engaged in other activities so that what they eat barely registers with them at all. Eating mindfully is the exact opposite of the zoned-out eating or eating on the run that are now so popular. Fifty years ago it would have been a rare sight to see anyone eating anything except when seated at a table. The modern widespread habit of walking along the pavement eating fried chicken from a cardboard box would simply never have happened, and the whole takeaway food culture was then in its infancy. In many ways we were a fitter, leaner people when eating took place in a more formal setting.

Just a couple of generations back, food was cooked from scratch with fresh ingredients and served at a table in the family's dining room or kitchen. If you think it is progress that you need never cook food for yourself, and just ping something in the microwave, we would like you to reconsider your view.

However, for now we want you to understand that whatever your food choices, it is important both physiologically and psychologically to be more aware of when you eat. When you prepare food and cook it, all your senses are engaged, and they send messages to your brain that food is on its way. The brain in turn sends messages to your digestive system to stimulate production of enzymes necessary for optimum digestion.

The body also responds well when it regularly goes through times of eating, and times of not eating – in other words, regular mealtimes as opposed to constant grazing throughout the day. With regular meals two or three times a day, you learn how your body feels when it is hungry, and how your body feels when it is replete. Clients who constantly graze on food tell us that they are confused about when they are hungry and find it difficult to tell when they are full so they just eat all day long.

We recommend you apply some of the key principles of mindful eating to your own meals:

If you usually eat lunch at your desk, make it a rule to eat somewhere else in your workplace instead, or better still, take a break away from the office or factory to be in the open air if possible. We understand the pressure of 'presentism' in the modern workplace, so even if leaving your desk for an hour would be radically against your workplace's culture, then just a 20-minute break away would be a positive improvement to your wellbeing and your day. If you do have to stay at your desk or work station to eat your lunch, turn off any screens or dim down their brightness to minimise distractions.

If you usually eat your meals at home on your lap while sitting on the sofa watching television, try eating at a table instead. If that's not possible, at least for the duration of your meal turn off the distraction of the television and focus on what you are eating. Mindless eating while watching TV or surfing the net makes it easy for you not to recognise the messages your stomach sends to your brain to tell you when you are full, making it all too easy to overeat.

You may live with other family members where everyone is used to collecting their food from the kitchen at different times, and even eating it alone in their rooms. Instigate the eating of one meal a day, or even one meal a week, when all the family comes together to share the experience of eating together. If the family mealtimes of your childhood were stressful, you could break that pattern with your own family. Mealtimes can be an opportunity to share news and catch up with each other over good, simple food.

Eating quickly is also at odds with optimum health and the principles of mindful eating. Try to chew each mouthful until the food is properly broken down before swallowing. Many people under-chew their food, swallowing pieces that are impossible to digest properly. Even if you are eating nutritionally-rich food, your body's digestive system would struggle, and probably fail, to extract the full nutrient content from large chunks of food.

A good habit to adopt while you consciously slow down your eating is to follow the mantra of 'mouth full, hands empty'. This means putting your cutlery down between mouthfuls and only picking it up again when you have chewed and swallowed the previous mouthful. This will make eating a meal a much slower experience, and you will find you will almost definitely be content to eat less than you would usually.

A common, mindless sort of eating is eating leftovers from your children's plates as you clear away. Implement a rule to scrape all waste food into the bin. If you are hungry, then you need to eat a proper meal, preferably your own proper meal. If you have issues around wasting food, and it feels challenging for you to throw food away, then refer to the previous section in the book on PSTEC and leaving food on your plate (page 118) for guidance on how to clear that particular block.

Finally, whatever you eat, serve it wherever possible on a plate while you are seated at a table. Focus on the act of giving your body nutrition. Give your body the best nutrition you are able to provide for yourself. Work on achieving this, one meal at a time. Look at your food; breathe in deeply its fragrance; take a moment to acknowledge that you are giving this nutrition to yourself with love; acknowledge that you deserve the best you can provide.

Emma's story

As told to the authors and included here with Emma's permission.

'When I started therapy I reckon I wanted to lose around two and a half stone (35 lb/16 kg), which isn't a lot when you think of how much some people want to lose, but it was the heaviest I'd been for a long time and I felt miserable, overwhelmed and tired of it all. I'd always been slim, skinny even as a child and teenager. I'd put on my weight in my 20s, carrying more with each of my three children. Somehow I always managed to claw myself back, but not quite to my former slim self.

'Over 20 years ago, when our children were small and I was coming up to my 30th birthday, my husband had an affair with someone at work.

Out of sheer bloody-mindedness, and revenge I guess, I got down to nine and a half stone (133 lb/60 kg) in under four months. It was an ego boost while it lasted, but basically my heart was broken. I had all this anger around his betrayal that I didn't know what to do with, so in the end, I just ate and ate.

'When I started therapy I was approaching my 50th birthday. I felt middle-aged and over the hill. I was also still full of anger. Fury just consumed me. It was like a big fist in my stomach and it felt like it had been there for years. The only way I knew how to calm myself down was to eat.

'My husband and I didn't split up over his affair. In fact, we hardly ever spoke about it. Twenty years later, when I first talked about him in my therapy sessions, I called him every swear word I could think of. Even our grown-up children knew I thought of him with total disdain and whenever I had the opportunity to put him down, or make him feel small, then I would. I was remorseless. When it had come to the crunch, he had chosen to stay with me and I was committed to being with him, but that didn't mean I wasn't beyond exacting my revenge for what he'd done by taking out all my fury and anger on him.

'When I was asked if I wanted to split up with him, I was taken aback. I began to slowly acknowledge the truth to myself about how I loved the very bones of the man and how much sadness I carried in my heart that our relationship had turned out the way it had. My anger just covered all the pain I was in and the way I coped with it was to use the ways I had learnt growing up. I was raised in the kind of family where my Dad, and even my Granddad, were casually cruel to me, my brothers and my sister. I learnt very early on not to show any weakness. If I was hurting and they could see it, I'd just get more of the same. I also learnt very early on not to speak out because as far as they were concerned I didn't matter, or they would just use it as another opportunity to slap me down.

'Over time, I developed this impenetrable shell. I was as loving as anything to my own kids, but if I was crossed by a friend or a neighbour, then this hard front came down and they would be as good as dead to me. In therapy I came to see that these were strategies I'd developed to get me through my life. They sort of worked, but I paid a high price as it never felt safe for me to show my vulnerability, so everyone thought I was as hard as nails. All of my vulnerable feelings had to be swallowed down and that's what I did with food.

'As I worked in my therapy sessions, I learned to get in touch with and express the emotions I'd never felt safe to express before, and with that my eating came into balance. I started to lose weight and steadily got my weight down. With my husband it began to feel right to me that I showed him how much I loved him. I simply didn't need to punish him any more and the changes in our relationship have been remarkable and enduring. Glen is absolutely at the centre of my life.

'My weight loss hasn't been without its hiccups. In the last few years I've had some huge challenges to face that have thrown me back into some of my old behaviours and habits. My much loved sister-in-law has an inoperable brain tumour. We all watch pretty helplessly as she edges closer to her passing, which is hard to bear, especially for my brother and our extended family. My Dad survived my Mum by several years, and the last four years have been exceptionally difficult as my sister and I cared for him at his home while he fought cancer. To the end, not once did he miss an opportunity to undermine me, say something critical, or set my sister and me at odds with each other. He remained manipulative and unkind to his dying day. That makes me sad as I so wished it could have turned out differently. I think the little girl in me was really hoping right up to the end for an acknowledgement, a kind word, a gesture of love, but he just wasn't able to give that to me.

'These big life events certainly threw my eating into chaos for a while. In the past I would have responded with a downward spiral of binge eating that could have led to possibly months, or even years, of weight gain. Nowadays I recognise my old patterns and can interrupt them. It doesn't mean I don't sometimes feel overwhelmed with everything and sorry for myself, but I also understand that while my Dad couldn't love me, that was his loss. It was never about me. He was damaged. I understand now though that I can love me. That little girl inside of me is safe with me, and I'm never going to let her down.

'Key to me and Glen sorting out our marriage was me learning that Glen was not the same as my Dad. When the betrayal happened I was triggered into old responses I'd learnt from my Dad. The emotional bullying, the lack of tenderness, were just learnt habits that I used to hide behind. As I got more in touch with my real feelings the more I was able to share them with him again. He made a mistake, we both know that, and he chose to stay with me so what was the point in letting it eat me up, or even fatten me up, to ruin our chance of a happy life together? My opening up to him has been the most wonderful happening in my life and we are closer than ever.

'I've figured out other stuff too that used to make me feel dreadful about myself and would trigger me to emotionally overeat. Glen has times when he needs to withdraw a bit. Sort of man-cave stuff. Maybe it's work or something else he's trying to get his head around, but I realise now that it's not a judgement about me. It's his stuff and I can let him be and I'm still fine. It's a huge relief. Also, I used to really resent that I was the family's social secretary, holiday co-ordinator, forward planner and generally the one the buck stopped with. I used to want him to be different, to step up. The truth is, it's not his way and I'm good at it. I've found peace with who he is, and who I am. When I think back to how our marriage was, it is like someone else's life and I'm so glad it's not mine.

'A while back I did lose over 23 pounds (10.5 kg) and I felt and looked amazing. I've put a bit of that back on in the last year just because life got in my way, but I know exactly what to do to let those extra pounds go and they really can go now. If I catch myself soothing myself with food I can say to Glen, "Can I have a hug?", and he's always happy to oblige. My life is better than I thought – better than I dared hope for.'

Step Three: Body image

Heal the source of your self-hatred

Our bodies bear testament to our lives. Carrying excess weight is a manifestation of a body out of balance. Your work is to bring yourself back into balance so that it is safe to release the excess weight and achieve your natural weight. The goal is to feel at home and safe in yourself – to honour and care for yourself to the best of your ability and to end self-punishing and self-sabotaging behaviour.

It is helpful now to acknowledge how little we are at peace with ourselves by writing down as many of the negative, and positive, judgements you make about your looks and your own body on the next worksheet. By shining a light onto your self-critical, self-assassinating beliefs you can take the first step in taking back your power.

The worksheet is the place to list all the things you like about your body and all the things you dislike. Use the words you, or others, have used to describe you physically. Write down the praise and the admonishments.

As you do this, make a note of any emotions, or memories that surface. As always, take your time with this. We carry the weight of our own self-criticism, and bear the emotional load of harsh words, and the physical trespasses others have made against us.

Here are some examples of like, and dislike, from other clients.

The 'like' list
- 'I like my eyes.'
- 'My ankles are slim.'
- 'I have narrow wrists.'

The 'hate' list
- 'My breasts get me too much attention.'
- 'I am never strong enough to protect myself.'

Love and hate

- 'I hate my big stomach.'
- 'Being small means being weak.'

To download the A4 printer-friendly pdf version of the 'Love and hate' worksheet, go to www.your7simplesteps.com and click on the Worksheets tab.

Resolve self-loathing with EFT

EFT set-up for first tapping round

'Even though I hate my body and myself, I completely and fully love and accept these feelings.'

'Even though I'm disappointed in myself that I haven't managed my eating better in the past, I completely and fully love and accept myself as I am now.'

'Even though it's too late to turn this around and I'm hating myself for being such a failure, I'm willing to learn to completely and fully love and accept myself without judgement.'

First, take three fairly deep and gentle breaths. Breathe in through your nose and softly out through your mouth. Don't use any force or pressure.

Now focus for a moment on your breathing and assess the degree of your self-loathing. Give this a SUD rating with zero signifying you are completely at peace with your physicality and 10 signifying the highest degree of self-loathing.

First round of tapping

EB: 'I'm so tired of hating myself.'
SE: 'There's nothing to love about me.'
UE: 'There's nothing to love about my body –
N: 'it looks disgusting.'
C: 'There's nothing to love about me or my body.'

CB: 'I'm totally unlovable.'
RIBS: 'It feels too hard to change now.'
UA: 'It's all too late.'
W: 'I'm so disappointed in myself.'
TH: 'I'm such a failure.'

Pause. Take one easy, deep breath.

EFT set-up for second tapping round

'Even though I still feel like a dismal failure, I completely and fully love and accept myself.'

'Even though I'm believing that it's too late to change, I completely and fully love and accept myself as I am now.'

'Even though I'm struggling to get past this self-loathing, I completely and fully love and accept myself without judgement.'

Second round of tapping

EB: 'I'm such a failure.'
SE: 'I've never been good enough and my body is evidence of this.'
UE: 'It hurts so much to feel these feelings...
N: '...of self loathing.'
C: 'I'm so tired of feeling this way.'
CB: 'I only notice everything that is wrong with me and my body.'
RIBS: 'What if I could start noticing the things that are right,
UA: 'and feel grateful for them.'
W: 'There are things that are great about me and my body and I'm starting to notice these.'
TH: 'I'm learning to tell better stories about myself and my body.'

Pause. Take one easy, deep breath. Assess your level of self-loathing and rate it again from zero to 10.

EFT set-up for third tapping round

'Even though I'm still just learning to feel better about myself and my body, I completely and fully love and accept myself.'

'Even though I am carrying all these stories in my head about myself and my body, I'm willing to start telling better stories and I completely and fully love and accept myself as I am now.'

'Even though parts of me still struggle to love and accept me just as I am, I'm willing to give my body some love and support as I learn new ways of thinking and behaving.'

Third round of tapping
EB: 'All these old stories in my head.'
SE: 'I made them all up.'
UE: 'They're not even true, so I'm choosing to let them go.'
N: 'I'm starting today to make these changes in my thinking.'
C: 'As I let go of all these old beliefs and stories that have been keeping me stuck,
CB: 'I'm learning to be grateful for myself and my body.'
RIBS: 'My body takes care of me in so many wonderful ways, and I'm learning to love my body and be grateful for it.'
UA: 'Releasing these old stories now...'
W: 'feeling better and better and better with every new day...'
TH: 'loving myself more and more every day!'

Pause. Take one easy, deep breath.

Assess your level of self-loathing again, giving it a SUD rating from zero to 10.

If the SUD rating is still middling to high repeat the first tapping round if required to further reduce your SUD rating.

Resolve self-loathing with PSTEC
So you look into a mirror and see your body. What is your initial reaction? Most times it may be disgust – or revulsion. It's quite rare that people carrying excess weight can view themselves in the mirror and feel okay about

their bodies. The problem with hating our bodies, however, is that when we are feeling so much shame and disgust at how terrible we look it's almost impossible to shed that excess weight. Such a paradox! PSTEC (see page 39) is really effective for this problem. Think about your body. What is the part that disgusts you the most? Your thighs? Your stomach? Your arms? Give this disgust (or hatred) a number out of 10. Start your work on the part that has the highest intensity. Get that feeling up as high as you possibly can.

Now, use the click track (see page 186) to start clearing this feeling. When the track has finished, check and reassess the intensity of your disgust. This should have started to decrease. Continue repeating the click track until you have reached a zero and when you think about this part of your body there is no emotional intensity at all.

Now move on to the remaining parts of your body that disgust you. Choose the one that produces the highest intensity of disgust and clear that feeling. Continue until you are totally void of any negative feelings as you see yourself in the mirror.

What your fat says for you and to you

Imagine if your fat could speak; what would it want to say to you? Here is a wonderful and intuitive way to find out. This is a guided meditation, and its effectiveness, and the power of the insights you can receive, are totally dependent on your willingness to just go with the process and play with it imaginatively. The playfulness of the process is to allow feelings, images, colours and sounds to come to your mind. It is a stream-of-consciousness technique so do not impose rules or limitations on your imagination. It is important not to judge your responses or impose real-life logic on them. Give yourself time with this.

The way people perceive and conceptualise information falls into three main categories. They are visual (what you see), aural (what you hear) and kinesthetic (what you feel), so your responses to your exploration may be mainly the sights you can see, or the sounds you can hear or the emotions you feel.

- Find some time when you will not be disturbed. Sit comfortably, or lie on a bed if you are confident you will not fall asleep. Make sure you are cosy.
- Stroke your body. Get in touch with the landscape of you. The hilly parts, and the valleys, until you feel you are experiencing your body in all its fullness.
- Imagine the index finger of either hand has a light at its tip. You can conjure up a light that most appeals to you. It could be a glowing ember, or a flame, a shard of crystal, or the brightest torch light. Whatever light you have made for yourself, make it bright so that it casts a powerful light.
- Take your index finger with its light attached and push it gently against an easily accessible part of your anatomy that you feel pretty neutral about, for instance your forearm. Women often have strong feelings about their breasts, or thighs or belly, but for this first part of the process, choose a section of your anatomy that you do not have strong feelings about.
- Use the light on your index finger to illuminate inside the part of your body you are focusing on. In this case, if it is your forearm imagine the light spreading throughout your limb from the wrist all the way to your elbow. Let that light illuminate every nook and cranny it can find.
- Use your imagination to see, hear and feel everything that is being illuminated. Ask yourself, 'What can I see? What can I hear? And what emotions are held here?'
- When you feel you have given yourself ample time to fully explore your chosen environment, it is time to carefully extract your light by withdrawing your index finger, making sure the light stays attached to its tip.
- Take a moment to refresh your light. If it is a glowing ember then blow on it to reignite it, or if it is a shard of crystal then polish it so that it shines as brightly as possible.
- Now is the time to press your index finger against a very different part of your body. It is now time to choose a part of you that you are particularly unhappy with – the part of you that most represents to you your overweight or fat state. We have found most people focus their self-loathing on their stomach or thighs.
- Press your index finger against your flesh and again allow your light to enter and illuminate this new area. Let your light spread as far as you can

see. The internal scale is completely imaginary. People have visualised vaulted ceilings, cavernous empty spaces or complex canal systems. Again it is worth emphasising that this is something apart from logic and will work most favourably when you suspend all restrictions on your imagination.

- Take your time to find how your fat is visualised on this guided journey. What does it look like? Consider colours and texture. What sounds does your fat make? What feelings are in your fat? Ask your fat what it wants to say to you and what it needs you to know.
- Take the time to really explore these important messages and insights.
- Once you have spent ample time exploring the messages from your fat, ask it what it needs you to do or to understand so that it can be released. Ask it and wait for its reply. It can reply in an image, sound or feeling. Stay with this until you have clarity. It is important again not to judge its reply but to acknowledge it.
- Finally, choose a powerful healing colour for yourself and imagine it at the top of your head and travelling down throughout your body. In your healing colour there is an understanding and love for yourself.
- Let the healing colour flood throughout your body, intensifying wherever additional healing and self-forgiveness are required.
- Send a message to your fat that you have heard everything it needs you to know and it can go now – that it is safe for it to go.
- Breathe and let go.

Steps to acceptance and moving on

By the time you have reached this stage of the book our hope is that you will have developed a greater understanding of your particular type of emotional eating. The depth of your insight is dependent on your having taken the time, and had the commitment, to apply yourself to the various self-discovery tasks along the way. It is by understanding the triggers to your eating emotionally, and fully resolving and releasing these, that you can stop the problem.

You will have worked for instance on your old limiting self-beliefs to the point where there is now no emotional load attached to memories or events that previously would have triggered you to eat emotionally. If you are still aware of pockets of resistance, then take your time to revisit earlier sections of the book so that you can make sure you have resolved and released any old issues around food. Do not be disappointed if resistance is still showing up or worry you will never resolve your issues. Each time you notice resistance to letting go and making changes is a gift as it shows you where to focus your attention.

Release your fear of success

Fear of success can be as big a stumbling block to achieving your dreams as fear of failure. What does success mean to you? Now is an opportunity to discover how your fear of success could cause you to self-sabotage the weight loss you desire.

Initially you may think that there can be nothing at all negative about you achieving your weight-loss goal, and that it can only be positive. However, pause and take your time with this. Delve deeply. Allow your mind to drift. Perhaps when you really think of reaching your goal weight you may find you are harbouring some misgivings about actually achieving this goal.

See yourself at your goal weight. Imagine how that feels. Bring all your senses into play so that as you visualise yourself you can powerfully feel how it would be.

Now, see yourself in different places and situations with different people:

How does staying at home feel?
How does going out feel?
How do strangers respond to you?
How do members of the opposite sex respond to you?
Are friends and family the same with you or is their behaviour different?
What does it feel like going to your studies or to work at your ideal weight?

Fear of success

If you have been at this weight before, what was that like? Did
anything negative happen?
Who will be happy for you?
Who will feel threatened by your weight loss?
Who will expect more of you?

Is there any inkling of unease? Having tried for so long to achieve the weight
loss you desire it may be surprising to discover any negativity around actually
achieving the reality of it.

These uncomfortable feelings need to be cleared or they will encourage
self-sabotaging behaviour around food, including emotional eating that
has got in your way in the past. Use the next worksheet to explore any
misgivings you have. Note them down. Allow yourself to get in touch with
any uncomfortable feelings of what you and/or your life might be like for
you at your goal weight.

*To download the A4 printer-friendly PDF version of the 'Fear of success'
worksheet, go to www.your7simplesteps.com and click on the Worksheets tab.*

EFT script for ending your fear of success

EFT set-up for first tapping round
'Even though I'm fearful of my success, I completely and fully love
and accept myself.'

'Even though I'm not deserving of success, I completely and fully love
and accept myself as I am now.'

'Even though success feels really scary to me as I certainly don't
deserve it, I completely and fully love and accept myself anyway
without judgement.'

First, take three fairly deep and gentle breaths. Breathe in through your nose
and softly out through your mouth. Don't use any force or pressure.

Now focus for a moment on your fear of success and give it a SUD rating with zero signifying no fear and 10 signifying feeling really fearful.

First round of tapping

EB: 'I don't deserve success.'
SE: 'I always sabotage any progress I make.'
UE: 'I'm not worthy of success.'
N: 'I don't deserve success.'
C: 'I don't feel safe deserving success.'
CB: 'I never have.'
RIBS: 'I can't change these patterns.'
UA: 'I'm not worthy of success.'
W: 'I just don't feel safe being successful.'
TH: 'I can't change that now.'

Pause. Take one easy, deep breath.

EFT set-up for second tapping round

'Even though I still have this fear of success, I completely and fully love and accept myself.'

'Even though I'm afraid that success will just create opportunities for me to fail, I completely and fully love and accept myself as I am now.'

'Even though I would rather sabotage my success than fail one more time, I completely and fully love and accept myself without judgement.'

Second round of tapping

EB: 'I can't fail anymore.'
SE: 'Success feels too scary for me.'
UE: 'I can't stand any more painful failures.'
N: 'I don't think success is safe for me.'
C: 'I've had too many failures in my life.'
CB: 'I wonder if it's possible to start releasing this fear,
RIBS: 'because it's keeping me so stuck,
UA: 'but I worry that I shall just fail again.'

W: 'I'm so stuck in these bad habits,
TH: 'but I really want to succeed this time.'

Pause. Take one easy, deep breath.

Assess your fear of success and rate it again from zero to 10.

EFT set-up for third tapping round
'Even though I'm still feeling a little scared of success, I completely and fully love and accept myself.'

'Even though I am afraid of moving forward, I'm open to letting go of this fear now and I completely and fully love and accept myself as I am now.'

'Even though I've been stuck for so long feeling fearful of success, I now forgive myself and I forgive this fear.'

Third round of tapping
EB: 'I choose to release this fear now.'
SE: 'I choose to be brave and move forward easily.'
UE: 'I have decided to be courageous.'
N: 'As I release those old limiting fears,
C: 'I choose to accept that success is safe for me.'
CB: 'A part of me knows I can do this.'
RIBS: 'I know I can reach my goal.'
UA: 'I won't give up.'
W: 'I can choose success.'
TH: 'This time I'm choosing success.'

Pause. Take one easy, deep breath.

Assess your level of fear of success and rate it from zero to 10. How close to zero are you?

Repeat the first tapping round if required to further reduce your SUD rating.

Release old memories of being judged with PSTEC

Do you have memories from your past – even your childhood – of being judged? Were you the fat kid? Were you too embarrassed to get undressed in the changing-rooms? Did a nurse comment on how you should lose some weight... in front of all the other children? So you went home and emptied the fridge or pantry to try and dampen down the humiliation you felt?

Sit down in a quiet place and let your mind wander back to those times. Make a list of all those experiences that felt so uncomfortable. Keep writing until they're all down in front of you. Now rate each of those experiences with a SUD rating out of 10, with 10 being the most intense and zero being no negative feelings.

Using the click track (see page xx), start to clear these experiences. Begin with the experience that has the highest score for intensity. Run the click on it ensuring that as you're listening to the audio you keep the emotional intensity as high as you possibly can. When the track has finished, check to see what number you are scoring now for this experience. The intensity should have started to decrease. Continue repeating the click track until you have reached zero so that when you recall that experience there is no emotional intensity remaining at all.

Now move on to the other experiences. Choose the one with the next highest intensity and clear the emotions associated with that one. Continue with the remaining experiences. You will probably find that after you've cleared the really intense ones, the ones lower down will just drop away and have no emotional intensity at all.

Check in your mind and see if you have any more recent experiences that still feel raw. Make sure you clear those as well.

How 'afformations' create powerful change

Affirmations (with an 'i') only work occasionally because they often cause doubts in our mind. This is because we are often trying to convince our mind of something we may not really believe to be true.

Noah St John developed the concept of afformations (with an 'o') based on the theory that rather than telling our mind what we want and then hoping that we can overcome any resistance we experience, we should ask a question so that our mind will automatically begin searching for an answer to the question.

Do make sure that you ask empowering questions – disempowering questions such as *'Why am I overweight?'* tell us that we can't do anything right. Because we always manifest what we focus on, if we ask negative questions we get negative results. So you must ensure that your afformations are always positive and the results can be amazing.

After each afformation, repeat the word 'Yes' about 10 times.

Use the afformations often during the day and you should start noticing a change within 14 days.

Here are some examples:

'Why do I find it so easy to follow a healthy, balanced diet?'
'Why is it so easy to reach my natural target weight?'
'Why do I treat my body so well?'
'Why do I let go of these excess pounds so easily?'
'Why do I not allow negative thoughts to live in my mind?'
'Why do I see my body perfect just as it is?'
'Why do I look in the mirror and see I am enough?'
'Why do I forgive my past mistakes?'
'Why do I love my healthy lifestyle?'
'Why do I have the perfect shape for me?'

Remember you can write your own afformations. Your own words are always more powerful than anyone else's.

Lorraine's story

Lorraine tells her story of a lifetime's struggle with food and weight issues and how she found a peaceful resolution as she approached a key crossroads in her own life.

'I have fought weight problems all my life, coming from a family where borderline eating disorders were the norm and eating, or not eating, was a way of taking control in a rather unhappy household.

'Despite a happy marriage and having raised two wonderful, now adult, children, my problems reared their ugly head again – big time.

'I felt I was fat and at 58 years of age, at a crossroads in my life – what was to become of this overweight and therefore unattractive woman now, whose children needed her less?

'On top of all that, I was also experiencing difficulties in having my widowed mother living nearby in a residential care home, from where she would still exercise an emotional power over both me and my younger sister.

'I was the heaviest I had ever been in my life at over 16 stone (224+ lb/102+ kg). I had it in my mind that I wanted to travel with my husband to Israel to celebrate my 60th birthday. The reason I wanted to be slimmer for the trip was that I had strong recollections of all the times I had gone there as a single, and more attractive (as I thought), young woman. The last time I had visited had been in June 1985, on my own for work. At that time I had been married for only about 10 months. I now wanted to go back there *as that same woman*, albeit much older, more experienced, with a husband and grown children, but not looking completely unrecognisable from the outside. I was not expecting to see anyone that I'd known back then, but it was just something I had in my mind. I wanted to feel proud of myself, and losing weight was going to be the tangible proof of that.

I've dabbled with different forms of therapy for over the past 25 years, but hadn't found anything remotely effective for more than 20 years.

By lucky chance I came across this programme on the internet and booked several one-to-one sessions. I have to tell you the location of these sessions was literally miles away from me, right across town, so not the easiest of journeys, but as it turned out, so, so worth the effort! I've learnt so much about myself and my triggers to emotional eating. I've come to understand and recognise my catastrophic thinking, something I had become very good at with years of diligent practice.

'My default setting when faced with challenging changes, or what I catastrophically perceived to be challenging changes, was for my subconscious to attempt to pre-occupy me with more benign thoughts, and for me these often centred around food, or sometimes around domestic arrangements or decisions. It's a sort of side-ways strategy I had unconsciously developed to avoid having to deal with real issues that were bothering me. I could fool myself that I wasn't feeling anxious at all by focusing on, and over-thinking, the small stuff, and just eat and eat instead.

'My resistance to letting go of my old coping strategies has been a challenge. The old, old question, "Who would I be if I wasn't thinking about food?" or, "What would I need to address if my head wasn't full of all this over-thinking?" kept me stuck for a long time and can still be my knee-jerk response when faced with big, unwelcome changes in my life. Nowadays though, I recognise them for what they are – just old fears and patterns of behaviour. In the past, I would have plummeted into a spiral of binge eating or secret eating and that doesn't happen now. I recognise when something is out of kilter and I can gently explore what is going on in my life and reassure myself in ways that do not involve soothing myself with food.

'PSTEC and EFT worked really well for me as methods of collapsing and resolving my emotional drivers to overeating. Both techniques seem really weird but they help – a lot.

'I gained insights about myself so that when I am triggered by changes in my life and plunged into my default anxiety response of obsessing about food, I can choose other, more productive and certainly less fattening responses instead. I learnt to acknowledge all of the changes I had already faced and dealt with in my life – in fact, just being able to acknowledge to myself that life is perpetually changing and never static, has been strangely comforting.

'I had never given myself credit for all that I had achieved with my life, and with my family, and although I'm not a natural at patting myself on my back, or even properly listening when people compliment me, I do get it now that I am a very capable, good person, who really does try to do her best. I'm kinder to myself for sure, which feels revolutionary and a huge relief.

'By the time my 60th birthday rolled around I had, indeed, achieved my weight-loss goal and had lost five stone seven pounds (77 lb/35 kg). I felt absolutely marvellous and it was a truly memorable holiday. Now, some two years later, I can say I even lost a little more weight at one stage and have since put a little back on. My weight loss nowadays is stable at just under the five stone mark (70 lb/32 kg) and has been for a long time. I would like to lose a little more, but it doesn't have the same urgency that it used to have. All I do know is that I am not going back to those old days of carrying all that extra weight. I feel liberated from the bingeing that had so taken over my life, and I now have the time and the emotional energy to think and do other things with my life.

'For me, it has not been about a "one-off cure". It has been about equipping myself with the right tools, together with learning to trust in myself that I am enough and I can deal with anything life throws at me. That doesn't mean I might like all the changes that happen, or that they don't feel like challenges, but I feel more able to deal with them nowadays and for that I am very grateful.'

Step Four: Setting and achieving your goals

Setting and achieving goals for yourself is a very important part of this programme. So, what's the best way of doing this?

Firstly, goals should not be too big. If you're currently over 31 stone (440 lb/200 kg), it's unwise to set an initial goal of reaching 11 stone (154 lb/70 kg). It will *feel* almost impossible and therefore very unlikely that you will be able to achieve it. Break your goal down to something more manageable and believable. As you reach the first stage you will find that you have much more faith in your ability to lose weight, and this helps keep you motivated as you move towards your ultimate target.

Don't forget to reward yourself when you attain your goals. Celebrate your success! This can be a simple 'pat on the back' or you may want to go out and buy yourself a new outfit.

People trying to lose weight are often prone to catastrophic thinking. They're on a diet and meet a friend for coffee. The cakes in the display are tempting and they buckle and have one. This then causes them to panic and the entire experience then becomes an absolute disaster in their mind. They then go on to escalate their thinking to tell themselves that they are failures... What's the point?... They might as well give up... It's all so hopeless... and they then go down into a destructive spiral. Not once will they have thought, 'Okay, that was delicious and now I'll go back to my healthy eating programme.'

Always make sure you keep perspective and focus on the bigger picture. One cake is not the end of the world if you have just managed three weeks of healthy eating. Practise challenging your thoughts. You have many hundreds of thoughts during your day that you never act on, so why can't you do the same with thoughts about food?

If a thought about chocolate comes into your mind, then stop and consider what is really happening. You may have a belief that you are addicted to chocolate. The reality is you just have an obsessive mind and don't know how to stop it! Ask yourself, 'Do I really need this chocolate?' Unless you're hungry, the answer is 'No', so brush the thought away and go and do something else. This could be making a cup of tea, patting the dog or phoning a friend – anything so that you forget about the chocolate. You will find that the thought has disappeared and you stay on track with your eating.

Remember that you have been thinking in these ways for a long time so it takes practice to learn new behaviours.

> *To download the A4 printer-friendly Weight loss log PDF go to www.your7simplesteps.com and click on the worksheets tab.*

Discover true motivation

What are your beliefs about physical fitness and wellbeing? Do you have opinions about people who put great store in taking care of themselves physically? You can bet you do. There is space on the next worksheet for you to tune in, listen and write out your own beliefs. Also, while taking the time to really listen to your beliefs, can you identify whose voice or attitude they are mimicking?

Here are some examples of beliefs clients have shared.

- 'Only jocks exercise. I'm too intelligent for that.'
- 'I've left it too late to get fit.'
- 'People would laugh at me if I went to a gym.'
- 'Only vain people exercise.'
- 'Only stupid people exercise.'
- 'Working out is boring.'
- 'I don't have the time to get fit.'

Take your time to explore what you really think about the kind of people

Blocks to wellbeing

who exercise regularly. What are your beliefs about joining a gym, turning up in your gym kit and taking part in physical exercise? If you have any negative opinions and feelings about these kinds of people, then you will be resistant to getting fit. Whose voice do these negative thoughts remind you of?

To download the A4 printer-friendly PDF version of the 'Blocks to wellbeing' worksheet, go to www.your7simplesteps.com and click on the worksheets tab.

Motivation increase with EFT

You can use EFT to clear your resistance to exercise and to increase your motivation to get fitter and healthier.

Use aspects of your blocks to wellbeing to compose an EFT script to clear your beliefs. Download and print out the EFT script template below if you want to formally compose your set-ups to increase your motivation. Alternatively, you can focus on your beliefs about exercise, or even your thoughts about the kind of people who regularly take part in exercise, and just begin tapping.

Remember tapping is a kind of ad-libbing or stream of consciousness, and a whole tapping round only takes under a minute, so there is no need to be hung up about making your set-ups ultra perfect. Also, the whole act of tapping encourages you to get in touch with your underlying feelings. Focus on your feelings about exercise and allow yourself to really feel your emotions so that they have a high SUD rating. Begin to see whether you can track back those feelings, following the thread of familiar feelings to take you back to earlier memories or events.

As we have mentioned previously, working with EFT can feel a lot like peeling back the layers of an onion, and if you are willing to just see where the process will take you, it is a powerful tool for revealing core events and memories that block you in the present day. You may begin with a set-up similar to one of the two below that feels fairly neutral, and see where it takes you.

'Even though I think exercise is really boring, and I just don't have the time to do it, I really do want to embrace good health so I'm ready to think of this differently.'

Repeat the set-up three times, or:

'Even though I know I'll feel healthier if I do some exercise, I'm not designed for any exertion and I'm just not going to do any!'

Repeat the set-up three times.

Tap a couple of rounds on 'Exercise is really boring' as your reminder phrase, or 'I'm not designed for any exertion'. Really listen to yourself saying the words, and explore how you feel below the surface of your words. Pause and breathe. Is that it? Is there something else half-hidden and unacknowledged just beneath the surface? If you can't get in touch with whatever it is that is blocking you, then you can tap a couple of rounds where you just take a breath as you tap on each point and see what else comes into your conscious mind. Perhaps a memory or event will begin to come into sharp focus, and then you can tap a round or two of EFT on that aspect.

Give yourself time to explore all aspects of your blocks to motivation to exercise until your SUD rating is down to zero and you are able to go to the gym or take up a physical activity of your choice.

To download the A4 printer-friendly PDF version of the 'Blocks to wellbeing' worksheet, go to www.your7simplesteps.com and click on the worksheets tab.

Increase your metabolism with EFT

What level is your metabolism functioning at right now? Let a number simply pop into your mind, or simply guess. It doesn't matter if you aren't 100 per cent accurate as we are only looking for a number that we can use later for a benchmark.

Now you can proceed with the first round of tapping. Start at the Karate chop point, or the sore spot (see page 28) and say:

> 'Even though my body runs at only … per cent, I deeply and completely love and accept my body without judgement.'

Repeat this statement three times.

Next, tap around on all the EFT points and repeat 'running at only … per cent'.

Now tap again on the Karate chop point or the sore spot and say:

> 'I choose to release anything and everything that slows my body down and I deeply and profoundly love and accept my body.'

Repeat this statement three times.

Then, tap on all the EFT points and repeat:

> 'Choosing to release anything and everything that slows my body down.'

Take a deep breath and then continue by tapping on the Karate chop point, or the sore spot, and saying:

> 'I now choose to repair everything that slows my body down and I deeply love and accept myself without judgement.'

Repeat this statement three times.

Then, tap on all the EFT points and repeat:

> 'Choosing to repair everything that slows my body down.'

Now take a new reading.

Keep repeating this process until you reach a number you're comfortable with.

Don't try to get your metabolism to work at 100 per cent on the first attempt.

Do a few rounds, perhaps once a week, as this will allow your body to adjust gently and easily into its new state.

To view a video sequence 'Using EFT to increase metabolism', go to www. your7simplesteps.com and click on the video sequences tab.

Release blocks to physical wellbeing with PSTEC

Does it feel overwhelming when you think about finding the time, or the necessary energy, to include regular exercise in your already busy life? Does it feel nigh on impossible to come home after a long day, and conjure up a nutritious meal for yourself? Does the idea of looking after yourself feel like the last thing you want to think about, at the end of a daily to-do-list that is already far too long? Is it a mystery to you how other people juggle the demands of their busy lives, and still have quality time left for themselves?

First, it will help enormously if you clear those feelings. When you are feeling overwhelmed, it is very difficult to even imagine how things can be different. Set yourself a SUD rating (see page 23), and run the PSTEC click track (see page 186) as you think about all the things you are expected to do in your busy day. Allow yourself to fully feel any resentment or anger that you have stuffed down inside yourself. Keep listening to the click track until you feel clear.

To ensure practical space in your life so that you can be a higher priority in your own life, you may need to review your own expectations. This could be how you are around the house, or in your job. It's time for you to put your health and wellbeing first, so it's helpful to let go of any unrealistic expectations you may have. The aim is not to worry quite so much if your house isn't always immaculate, or to feel relaxed about leaving work on time some evenings instead of staying late just to prove your dedication to the job.

Clear any anxiety you experience when you think about having a house that's slightly more untidy; or putting your coat on to leave work on time. Practise being healthily selfish by saying 'No' to a few duty, or boring, social engagements so that you have more time for yourself. Run the click track as you imagine these anxiety-inducing scenarios.

Also use PSTEC on the anxiety you feel when you imagine hearing yourself say 'No' to people, or to situations that leave you with no time to take care of yourself. Set a SUD rating for the anxiety in each situation at the outset, and make sure you get the intensity on all your scenarios right down to zero.

Formal exercise in a gym is certainly not to everyone's taste. What is the feeling you experience when you think about going for a brisk 30-minute walk? Is it dread? You can radically reduce dread by choosing a new activity that really appeals to you, or reviving a leisure activity you previously enjoyed. If you can combine exercise with something you enjoy, or might learn to enjoy doing, you will be much more likely to keep at it. If the thought of exercise, or taking up a physical activity, still feels abhorrent to you, then use the click track (see page 186) to clear your resistance.

Imagine yourself having to go for a walk. Or going to the gym. Or walking on that dusty treadmill that has been stored in the garage. What are the negative feelings? Write down as many as you can think of on the Blocks to wellbeing worksheet (page 148), and give each an SUD rating. Begin working with the click tracks on the ones with the highest intensity-score, until they are all down to zero. Soon you'll be wondering what all the fuss was about.

If you hate the thought of having to spend time cooking a meal from scratch using real food, then clear the emotions that you are feeling. If you have children, think about encouraging them to help with meal preparation. A client of ours has three children and now has the children chopping up the vegetables at dinner time. It's fun for them as they now enjoy the time together as a family. If the children are a little older, maybe you could encourage them to take turns in preparing an evening meal. They learn to cook, and you have a break! Find a way that works for you.

Brent's story

As told to the authors and included here with Brent's permission.

'When I signed up for therapy I was already on the waiting list for a gastric band operation. Major abdominal surgery was something I really wanted to avoid, so this programme really felt like my last-ditch attempt to get my weight under control.

'At the initial consultation, I weighed in at 24 stone and one pound (337 lb/153 kg). A week later, when I came for my first therapy session I topped that with an additional half a stone (7 lb/3 kg) for good measure. Those extra pounds were a classic "Last Supper" response, coupled with the fall-out from the celebrations for my 58th birthday.

'Clearly, I had a long way to go. I was under no illusions that my weight was causing me problems, but I was obviously not in the right frame of mind to fully focus on doing anything differently. Basically, I was disappointed in myself that I'd got myself in this state and felt pretty disgusted with myself for letting it happen. I had gone from being a well-built, strong athletic type of guy to someone who was classed as morbidly obese with painful joints, type 2 diabetes, high blood pressure and sleep apnoea. And, I felt like *I* had let all of that happen to me.

'All those negative opinions of myself are just great ways of beating myself up and keeping me stuck. Little by little I was able to let go of that self-blame and begin to do things differently.

'I'm a bloke so I like goals and structure. The first thing I did was set myself staged, with dated targets, towards my key goal of getting my weight down to 19 stone, 9 pounds (275 lb/124 kg). That wasn't an arbitrary weight by the way. That was the weight I needed to achieve to get myself out of the morbidly obese category as defined by the NHS [the UK's National Health Service] BMI (body mass index) measurement. I had to work hard to clear my self-doubts and to keep focused. When I began I was pretty overwhelmed and certainly didn't feel confident that I could make those changes happen. There were many two-steps-forward-and-one-step-backwards as I made progress towards my goal. For me, I really appreciated the hypnotherapy, and visualising myself achieving my goal weight really helped me to get there. In all, it took me just under a year to get down to the 19 stone 9 pounds target.

'The key for me appears to be a sort of mindfulness – not only during eating, but in keeping these issues, the decision to put my health first, the intention to be accountable to me, in the frame on a daily basis. This is what is difficult, because it is the opposite of what I have done all my life: putting personal issues on the back burner, but it is so good, and so successful, when I do it. And when you're on a roll success breeds success.

'I achieved my steadiest, most reliable, incremental, week-upon-week, weight loss when I listened to the hypno-recordings every day; kept a food diary; worked together with my wife to plan out the week's menu in advance; and we shopped for our meals and snacks so that everything was available in the kitchen. The food diary's weekly tally of my drinking prompted me to face up to, and then radically cut down, my alcohol consumption. That has stayed down ever since, as has switching regular take-away dinners for more home-cooked meals.

'I'd had a long belief that the "Bs" were responsible, and that cutting out Bread, Butter and Beer would do the job! However, just trying to cut out those with no mental support framework had in the past just been doomed to repeated failure, with each pound or stone off followed sooner or later with two back on! Now, the lowered carb diet that worked, and is mostly still working, for me does not demand forgoing butter – but, of course, the less I have the better (as Betty Botter might have said). Obviously Bread is out along with rice, pasta, chips, etc, and again, as my knees only allow me to perform limited exercise, Beer has to be off the menu.

'The quality of my mental support framework comes and goes. I find I am supported firstly by success and by personal relationships, the hypnotherapy CDs, and some sort of personal happiness index – what a list of variables.

'That might make it sound as though my weight loss was all down to practical factors, but of course key to all of this was me getting my head around the idea, the actual possibility, of me being able to lose the weight and that's what I did in the therapy sessions. I had so much doubt at my own ability to make a difference in my own life that for that first year I carried on attending the hospital appointments for the gastric band procedure, just in case I failed. I actually kept those appointments all the way up to when I no longer met the NHS's qualifying guidelines for surgical intervention. I had disqualified myself by no longer being fat enough!

'I found I really struggled to stay focused when I took on a couple of property renovations and my life got very busy and stressful. It became all too easy to let my health priorities take a back seat while I focused on working hard. I began making poor food choices, often eating on the run. That whole *mañana* thing of "I'll take care of myself tomorrow" had definitely been a bit of a theme for me for years, and had got me into the mess I'd already found myself in. Being busy again, and under pressure, triggered me into those old patterns of behaviour of not taking care of myself. The therapy sessions helped me realise I could make other choices for myself, that I mattered, and that taking care of myself mattered too.

'The four to five stone [56-70 lb/25-32 kg] I reduced my weight by had many welcome health benefits. The practice nurse at my GP [General Practice] surgery ran the statistics and said I had improved my life expectancy by 20 per cent. All of the readings from my regular blood tests were hugely better. My sleep apnoea had reduced from 40 interrupts per hour to initially 11 interrupts per hour, and now I keep meaning to return the breathing assistance machine to the hospital as I never need to use it at all, which of course is wonderful.

'I had a health scare last year driving back down to the south of England from Scotland with my wife. A few hundred miles into the trip I felt that tell-tale tightness in my chest and my heart was pumping nineteen-to-the-dozen. It was very scary. We were in a part of the country that we barely knew and had to make our way to the nearest hospital, where I was admitted for tests. I was eventually diagnosed with atrial fibrillation, a heart condition characterised by irregular heart beats which can lead to an increased risk of stroke, or even heart failure. I can't tell you how immensely pissed off I was. I had done everything I was told to do – eaten more healthily, cut down on the booze and lost weight and then – sod's law – this should happen to me. I felt all over again that my body had let me down. I know it's not rational but it's how I felt. I was back in that abyss thinking that I had allowed this to happen to me, that it was all my fault. It took a while to haul myself back up and really recognise that the weight I had lost had probably made the difference from being here today or not.

'I had got complacent, I guess. I thought I had done enough, but I have decided now I'm ready to lose the next chunk of weight. I've set a new weight-loss target. I've gone back to keeping a food diary and listening to the hypno-recordings every day. I want to build on the positive health improvements I've already gained and I'm keen to have more of the same. I'm talking to my wife about my plans as I know how well I can do when she and I work together, and she always loses some weight too so everyone's a winner!

'I understand now that I deserve to be well and happy and that no one can do that for me, except me, and I truly want that and I'm willing to work for it.'

Step Five : Breaking through

Let go and move forward

Are you feeling that your issues around emotional eating are now resolved and released? Are you now able to eat for nutrition instead of self-punishment? Have you explored every aspect of your resistance to change, and your secondary gains, and taken everything aspect down to a zero on the SUD rating?

Take time to sit and contemplate. Tap with a soft fist on your collarbone. Breathe and be open to what pops into your head.

- Is there anything else just below the surface?

- Is there anything half-formed in your mind – a shadow of something unspoken, something perhaps only partially acknowledged by you that may yet trigger you to emotionally eat?

- Are there any self-sabotaging behaviours you are holding on to?

- Do you feel any remaining anxiety when you think of yourself as slim and looking attractive walking down the street?

- Do you still have fears of what you could possibly lose in your life by being successful with your weight loss?

- Have you completed your work or have you merely come as far as you are willing, or able, to go?

- Are you doing everything you can to be successful, or are you holding back?

- What possible remaining benefits are there for you in failing at this?

Breaking through

These prompts are your final challenge. If you are clear of emotional blocks, you will know. If you have more to do to resolve and release your final, deeply buried issues, you will know that too.

You should by now be an expert in composing and ad-libbing your own EFT set-ups so now would be a good time to compose one based on anything that arises from this breaking-through step and then using PSTEC on any remaining negative feelings.

> *To download the A4 printer-friendly PDF version of the 'Breaking through' worksheet, go to www.your7simplesteps.com and click on the worksheets tab.*

Run-the-movie technique

Gary Craig, who was instrumental in developing emotional freedom technique (EFT) to be how we know it today, also invented the run-the-movie technique. You can use this EFT protocol, supported by the worksheet on page 161, with any painful memories that you carry with you in your life. You will always have the memories. They will not be deleted, but the link with uncomfortable emotions can certainly be reduced if not completely eliminated.

Take one of your early negative recollections of an event or situation that led you to emotional eating and write it out on the next worksheet as a two-minute movie script, beginning by giving it a title. If you have numerous memories, then choose the one with the most emotional heat still attached to it.

Tap with a soft fist on your collarbone and breathe as you do this. Condense the memory to a two-minute film — who was there, where did it take place and how did it make you feel?

Slowly read through your movie script. If/when you feel any uncomfortable emotion, then stop and give this discomfort a number from zero, which is equal to almost no discomfort, up to 10, which represents intense discomfort.

Run-the-movie

Pause and then tap full rounds of EFT on the discomfort you feel as you reach that point in your film script, until your have reduced the discomfort down to either zero or a very low number.

Check that you are emotionally clear by beginning again at the start of your script, and when you reach that uncomfortable point in your story again, the aim is to be able to read it without any increase of pain or distress. If this is the case, then continue reading until you reach the next part of your movie script that you find distressing as you recall it and then repeat the process until you have no emotional load left for your entire movie.

When you have completed that, apply PSTEC to the feeling of your whole movie narrative until you have collapsed any remaining emotional intensity.

To download the A4 printer-friendly PDF version of the 'Run-the-movie' worksheet, go to www.your7simplesteps.com and click on the worksheets tab.

Steps to acceptance and moving on

The depth of self-loathing and self-criticism associated with emotional eating can feel distressing. You are almost certainly harder on yourself than you would ever be on anyone else.

The processes described in this book will have revealed powerful insights for you to focus on and release. Use the guidance to compose your own tapping scripts using the tapping template to focus on self-love and self-acceptance. Work on the insights with the highest score of negative emotional intensity first as this often reduces, or collapses, the emotional intensity of the remaining ones.

Refer to the PSTEC section (see page 39) to formulate working with your key issues.

We have included some 'set-up' suggestions (see next) for EFT. Use them merely as inspiration on which to base your own work. Your own words are more powerful than anyone else's words. There is also no need to aim for perfection here. Use PSTEC and EFT to knock out the key issues that have emerged so far.

Keep checking back in with yourself. The easiest way to do that is the zero to 10 SUD rating, so don't forget to set a number for the related emotional intensity before you begin your work.

Relax. Breathe and let go.

'Even though I hate my body and the way I look, I accept myself as I am now even though it is really hard for me.'

'Even though I've been bullied and called names all my life, I am ready to speak to myself with kindness and care for myself with love and acceptance.'

'Even though I have hurt myself and damaged my health in my past, I am ready to bring healing to me.'

'Even though I find it hard to forgive everything bad that has happened to my body, I am tired of beating myself up and I'm ready to let go of all this guilt and self-blame.'

'Even though I am not used to taking care of myself, I am willing to begin today to treat myself better. It begins here and it starts with me.'

Melanie's story

As told to the authors and included here with Melanie's permission.

At 35 Melanie was the heaviest she had ever been. The previous five roller-coaster years had taken their toll on her waist-line, and her confidence. When she and her husband celebrated their fifth wedding anniversary they tucked their children aged four and two up in bed before slumping onto the sofa with yet another take-away, and bottle of wine.

'Sometimes I wonder where that ambitious young woman who had her career all mapped out and her life under control actually went. It's as though I've lost sight of her under all the effort of working full time and taking care of my girls,' she said as she began to explain her feelings. 'Everyone thinks I've made a great success of my life. Wonderful husband, beautiful children, and I'm really respected at work.' She paused. 'That's everyone except me. I'm terrified they'll find out I'm not as capable as they think I am, and my daughters will grow up to realise I'm a rubbish mum, or my husband will lose patience waiting for us to have some quality time together, and go off looking elsewhere.' Her eyes teared as she continued, 'Especially as I'm four stone [56 lb] heavier than when we got married and I can't even bear to have him touch me any more.'

Gently we began to unpick what was happening in her life, and especially what was happening for her around food. She talked about her comfort eating in her break times at work and eating sweets every evening in the car travelling to collect the children from their child-minder. 'I just crave sweet things. It's the only thing that keeps me going.'.

Working through the 'Timeline protocol' (see page 62), Melanie identified her reliance on sugary treats as beginning when she was 13 years old, when her family moved house and she moved from a small, rural school where she knew everyone to being the new girl at a much larger, city school. 'I've always been a bit of a swot. I loved learning, and putting my hand up in class to answer questions made me the target for a group of girls who made my life a total misery. I remember going home unhappy every day for what felt like ages and my mum being really off-hand with me. She said I was attention seeking and causing her and Dad more trouble. Dad had been made redundant, which was why we had moved, but I had no real idea what effect that was really having on our lives. Now when I look back I realise they must have been worried sick about money, plus Dad, who never really showed his feelings, got quite ill with depression around that time, which made things even harder for my mum.'

'Pretty soon I realised I was on my own. I became a bit of a chameleon at school. I remember making a conscious decision to fit in. I even trained myself out of my country accent. I stopped being a goody-two-shoes at school and sort of learnt to out-bully the bullies. I made myself fit in. Inside I still felt really lonely but I just kept that to myself. I started spending my lunch money on sweets and cigarettes with the other girls. If my mum or dad noticed any difference in me, they never said. When I noticed I was getting fatter I began messing about with laxatives and bingeing and purging sometimes, just like the other girls I was now friends with did. I carried on with that all the way through university.'

'Oh yes, I made it to university. Right at the last minute I knuckled down and passed my exams. Inside I was still the girl who loved learning. I had just learnt to keep that a secret too.'

'My boyfriend and I had only been going out together for about three months when I fell pregnant with our first child. We didn't have to get married, we just chose to. The way things worked out, we didn't even live together before the wedding. I suppose that was harder than I imagined. He wasn't brilliant at sharing how he felt. I used to joke with him that he was even quieter than my dad. We were only just getting used to each other when shortly afterwards we were getting used to being parents. It felt like we hadn't had a moment to really find out about each other, especially when I got pregnant with our second child so quickly.

'My secret eating and bingeing really kicked off again after our second child was born. Six months after the birth I went back to work full time with a brand new promotion as head of department at an inner city sixth form college. I thought I could manage everything and keep all the plates spinning. I never told my husband, Vic, how overwhelmed I felt; I just hid it all. I was worried that he might be feeling under pressure himself as he had changed from single man to married man and father of two in just a couple of years. I was also afraid that if I told him how I really felt he might think I was being unnecessarily dramatic, just like my mum had.

'So I just carried on with all my old coping strategies I'd developed when I was at school and university. I just kept all my emotions inside me, and drank way too much, and binged in secret whenever I had the chance. My mum broached the subject of me being under a lot of pressure during a shopping trip together. I must have been in a pretty bad way for her to risk saying anything to me.' She paused and momentarily laughed before becoming very serious again. 'Everything that should have given me so much joy just felt really hollow. Even my girls, who I adored, would be hustled through bathtime and bedtime with me in a bad temper so that I could get them out of the way and open a bottle of wine. I think my mum could finally see how unhappy I was. She had picked up a leaflet for Sally's clinic and she said she would pay for the sessions. I didn't even try to put on a brave face or deny anything. I think I knew I couldn't keep going on as I was, which is why I accepted I had to see someone and sort myself out. It's quite telling that although I could sort of admit to her that I needed help, I still kept the sessions secret from my husband for the first few weeks.

'Learning to use EFT [emotional freedom technique] I realised how high I had set the bar for myself with the type of job I was doing while at the same time taking care of two young children. Initially, it felt like a big deal for me to consider the possibility that I couldn't do it all. I also learnt in therapy how little of my own fears and doubts I had even admitted to myself, let alone shared with my husband. PSTEC [percussive suggestion technique] was brilliant in helping to free me from all those horrible old memories of being bullied at school, especially when no one at home wanted to listen to me. It was those old fears that I might not be listened to again when I really needed help that kept me from sharing how I felt with Vic.'

Melanie smiled broadly. 'I may have married Vic, but in all honesty I had never really allowed myself to rely on him. When I was able to say to him that my life was all a bit too much for me he really understood and heard me.' Melanie's face softened. 'I think our marriage properly began from around that time when I dared to share my real feelings with him.' She continued, 'In therapy I forgave myself for not being a super-mum and for relying on booze and rubbishy sweet stuff to keep myself going. Free from all that guilt I was able to go to my Head Teacher to speak with her about reducing some of my responsibilities.

Now, almost a year later even more changes have taken place. 'I'm back to my pre-marriage weight. I've lost over four stone (56+ lb), and I've cut my work down to three days a week. Vic and I have monthly date-nights when my mum and dad take the girls for a sleepover at their house. I don't drink at all during the week, and I don't even miss it!' She continued, 'I thought admitting to my Head of School that I couldn't cope would be the end of my career, but that hasn't been the case. I'm still ambitious, but I'm willing to take things more slowly now and enjoy these precious years with our daughters. I've also learnt that it's okay to ask for help. Vic is not my dad and I'm not that young girl any more who has to get by on her own. By asking for what I need I give myself the opportunity to be heard instead of stuffing it all down with crappy food, and I've also got closer to Vic as he gets to know the real me. I feel very lucky. I could scare myself if I dwelt for too long on how things might have turned out, but I'm too busy being happier to do that.'

Step Six: Digging deep

Explore and release remaining resistance

Now is the time to explore any remaining resistance to losing weight and being slim and healthy. Ideally, allow yourself ample time to sit and contemplate this part of the work. Tap with a soft fist on your collarbone. Breathe and, as usual, have a glass of water close by so you can stay well hydrated.

What self-sabotaging behaviours are you holding on to?

What fears do you retain when you think of achieving your natural weight?

What do you think you could lose in your life by being successful?

Have you come as far as you are going to go?
Are you doing everything you can to be successful or are you holding back?

What benefits are there for you to fail at achieving your natural weight?

To download the A4 printer-friendly PDF version of the 'Remaining resistance' worksheet, go to www.your7simplesteps.com and click on the Worksheets tab.

Try and work below the surface of your everyday thoughts. Write down whatever comes into your mind without necessarily getting too caught up with reading it back to yourself in the first instance. Be kind to yourself. Try not to judge yourself. This is the work that is left to do and acknowledging these last parts of resistance is the start to releasing them.

Release remaining resistance with EFT and PSTEC

PSTEC (see page 39) is wonderfully successful in reducing and collapsing all resistance to change. It removes the emotional pull that the thought of change can exert over you, leaving you feeling peaceful whenever you think about it. Moving out of your comfort zone can be very scary in many ways so we are looking to help you work through these fears easily, gently and quickly.

Think about losing all that excess weight. What pops into your mind? Is it your partner who will make things very difficult for you because he/she will feel so threatened that you are going to be looking great again? Was it the time you lost all that weight only to find you were getting huge amounts of attention at parties or get-togethers? Are you afraid that if you start looking amazing again you might be tempted to look outside your marriage for some fun? Are you remembering the time when you were small and weak and those children were bullying you – so you made a decision never to be small again? There could be any number of reasons as to why reaching your goal weight feels unsafe.

List any remaining fears on the next worksheet. Every last one of them. Now give each of those fears a SUD rating, with zero being no emotion at all, and 10 being the highest it can be.

Take the experience that feels the most intense and start working with that one. If it's a fear of what you think might happen in the future, it's perfectly okay to use that – imaginary experiences can be just as debilitating as real ones.

- Turn your phone off and go to a quiet place where you won't be disturbed.
- Now sit and think about that experience. Bring to mind all of the emotions... for example, being in the playground and those children

Remaining resistance

bullying and teasing you. Feel the fear and the powerlessness.

- On a scale from zero to 10, rate your feelings of fear and powerlessness. Zero is no emotion at all and 10 is the highest possible emotion.
- Run the PSTEC click track, following all of the instructions.
- So, you've done a round of the click track. Now, on a scale from zero to 10, rate the intensity of your fear and powerlessness. Zero is none at all and 10 is the highest possible. Has the number come down? Is it the same?
- If it's the same, just run the track through again. It should start coming down in intensity with the second round of the click track.
- Do ensure that you don't switch to another experience at any time when running the click track – just stay focused on the experience you began with. This process works best when you just concentrate on one experience at a time.
- If the emotional response has reduced, then make a note of your new number. Run the audio track again and continue to do this until you have reached a zero.
- Continue working through the experiences you listed, still working with the most intense ones. You will notice that the less intense experiences will start to drop away as the higher ones are cleared, so you probably won't have to work through all of them.

Step Seven: New day, new dawn

Become more intuitive

Take a big deep breath. Easy, nothing forced, and breathe out slowly. You've come so far, and we want you to reflect on the courage it has taken and remind you how proud you should be of yourself.

When you've been stuck for a long time, or been in the thrall of uncomfortable emotions that have ruled your life, it can feel very strange when those influences are no longer in control. Emotional eating has, in the past, taken the place of you speaking out or having your needs met. Having worked so hard to release and resolve your triggers to emotional eating, you may be wondering: what now?

Well, there is a part of you – a very powerful, wonderful part of you – that you have underused while you were swallowing down your emotions with food. This incredible part of you always works to promote your best interests and is your greatest advocate.

Are you intrigued as to what this part of you might be? Well, it is your intuition – your gut reaction. For some of you this will be tantamount to a formal introduction as this is not a part of you that you have ever acknowledged or even known existed.

Your intuition was drowned out with emotional eating and somehow got turned down and muffled under plates of food. Now, though, you are clear of all those emotional triggers, and it's time to meet your own very best friend.

Learning to hear your intuitive voice will take some practice. You will need to ask yourself questions, such as 'How do I feel about ...' whatever is bothering you, and wait for your intuition to answer. You may hear it or feel it. For most people, intuition is a feeling in their guts. When you are in touch with your intuition you recognise in real-time what it is telling you about anything that is happening to you, and the more you trust and value yourself, the more clearly you can hear your intuition respond, and then you can act accordingly.

Learn to say, 'I'll get back to you,' when people ask things of you. Even if everyone has been used to your being endlessly available in the past, from now on give yourself the opportunity of checking in with your intuition, and make a decision on how it feels for you.

You may have to take time to properly acquaint yourself with your intuition at the beginning. Think of it as a little like a muscle. You will need to familiarise yourself with it, use it often, and train it on different challenges, to get it up to full strength.

You can use EFT to help with this, and use a set-up similar to this to introduce yourself to your own intuition. Here is an illustrative suggestion as a set-up phrase:

> **'Even though I've never listened to my intuition in the past, and I'm not sure I know how to, I'm telling the universe now I'm listening, and I completely and fully love, and accept myself.'**

Say the set-up phrase three times.

Now, tap around all the EFT points. As you do so, alternate

> **'I don't know how to listen to my intuition' with**
> **'I am open to hearing my intuition.'**

Send the message that you are ready to hear, and gradually your intuition, instincts and insights will become clearer to you, guiding you towards what is best for your higher self.

Remember gratitude

Gratitude is one of the most profound emotions we can experience in our lives and yet we can so easily lose touch with things in our own lives that we feel true gratitude for.

Focusing on gratitude is also a powerful way for us to reinforce our desire to feel differently about ourselves and how we live our lives.

Our gratitude protocol asks you to write out 25 aspects of your life that you feel true gratitude for. Once you have your list, read through them and tap as you do. It is most powerful if you can do this last thing at night and first thing in the morning for at least seven days.

Below are 10 gratitude statements for you to begin with. Use the next worksheet (page 175) to copy these statements and add to them to record what else in your life you are grateful for:

'I am grateful for my desire to be slim and healthy.'
'I am grateful I am ready to forgive myself.'
'I am grateful for the love I have in my life.'
'I am grateful for surviving my past.'
'I am grateful that I can think of today with joy.'
'I am grateful for everyone I love.'
'I am grateful for the glorious sunshine today.'
'I am grateful I have embraced good health and wellbeing.'
'I am grateful I am taking better care of myself.'
'I am grateful for the good quality food I have in my fridge.'

Remember your own words are more powerful than anyone else's. The aim is to generate a minimum of 25 grateful statements

To download the A4 printer-friendly PDF version of the 'Gratitude list' worksheet, go to www.your7simplesteps.com and click on the Worksheets tab.

Gratitude list

Apex phenomenon

There is a well-documented response that sometimes happens with clients when they have truly resolved and released painful emotions around issues that had previously kept them stuck. It's called the 'apex phenomenon', which is a fancy way of saying what clients once thought was a big deal afterwards feels like a non-event when the therapist goes back and reminds them of their original presenting issues.

It is not unusual for a client to say , 'Oh yeah — my old flying thing', when actually they had originally come into therapy because they couldn't get on an aeroplane at all unless doped up to the eyeballs or in a state of profound anxiety. There was the woman who we asked, 'So, how are you about leaving food on your plate these days?' only to be met with a blank stare and a moment of confusion before she replied, 'Oh, yeah — I can do that now.' This is the very same woman who could never leave food on her plate as it had been drummed into her during her childhood that it was a sign of how wasteful and selfish she was in a world beset with poverty and starvation.

Anecdotes like this abound when working with clients with EFT and PSTEC. Through those techniques, the uncomfortable emotions are resolved and released, not buried or trained out of you. And, when those emotions are comprehensively released, then there is no residue left. Hence, the apex phenomenon.

Honour your journey

So, take the time now to go back through your worksheets and note book and check the notes you made as you worked through your issues. Notice your starting numbers and your finishing numbers. See how far you have come! Take the time to acknowledge your journey, and take pride in the profound shifts in your thinking and beliefs that allow you now to feel calm around food, to eat for nourishment and to stop emotional eating.

Chart your success

Your Seven Simple Steps programme is enhanced by marking your progress on the logs, checklist and food and mood diary we have specially designed for you to use while on the programme. You can download these for free at the web address below. Embrace your inner girl-guide or boy-scout, and get logging. You will record all that you've achieved and it will help spur you on to greater success.

Interestingly, doing this also highlights the parts of the programme you are finding challenging. You can then become aware of areas that could benefit from being further explored using EFT and PSTEC.

Logs available are:

Food and mood diary – Charting what you ate, when you ate and how you were feeling at the time can be very illuminating in the first week or so of your programme. It's not something you need to do forever, but we believe it's beneficial at the beginning. The food diary also asks you to assess how hungry you were when you wanted to eat, so this is an aid to unpicking what else may be going on for you. Emotionally that can get confused with a desire to eat.

Programme checklist – This is a chart format for you to tick your way along during your first 30 days to acknowledge everything you are achieving and the changes you are making in your life.

Attract weight release – This uses the powerful Laws of Attraction so that you can release those excess pounds effortlessly and easily. You are encouraged to adopt various practices, and embed habits that if undertaken consistently can result in an improved relationship with food as well as a positive effect on your weight. It's easy – just accumulate ticks in the right-hand columns to acknowledge completing specific daily actions and record your inevitable, steady weight loss in the left-hand columns. This format also works really well for ongoing successful weight maintenance.

Chart your success

*To download the A4 printer-friendly pdf of the 'Chart your success'
worksheet, go to www.your7simplesteps.com and click on the Worksheets
tab.*

Part Three

Your extra resources and downloads

References and sources

References

1 Ogden CL, Carroll MD, Kit BK, Flegal KM. Prevalence of childhood and adult obesity in the United States 2011-2012. *Journal of the American Medical Association* 2014; 311(8): 806-814.

2 Health & Social Care Information Centre (2014). Statistics on Obesity, Physical Activity and Diet.

3 Church D, Geronilla L, Dinter I. Psychological symptom change in veterans after six sessions of EFT (Emotional Freedom Techniques): an observational study. *International Journal of Healing and Caring* 2009; 9(1).

4 Church D, Feinstein D. Energy psychology in the treatment of PTSD: psychobiology and clinical principles. In: Van Leeuwen T, Brouwer M (Eds) *Psychology of trauma* 2013. Hauppage, NY: Nova Science Publishers; 211-224.

5 Karatzias T, Power K, Brown K, McGoldrick T, Begum M, Young J, Adams S. A controlled comparison of the effectiveness and efficiency of two psychological therapies for post-traumatic stress disorder: eye movement desensitization and reprocessing vs. emotional freedom technique. *Journal of Nervous and Mental Disease* 2011; 199: 372-378. DOI:10.1097/NMD.0b013e31821cd262

7 Feinstein D. Acupoint stimulation in treating psychological disorders: evidence of efficacy. *Review of General Psychology*, 2012; 16: 364-380. DOI:10.1037/a0028602

8 Salas MM, Brooks AJ, Rowe JE. The immediate effect of a brief energy psychology intervention (Emotional Freedom Techniques) on specific phobias: a pilot study. *Explore: The Journal of Science and Healing* 2011; 7: 255-260.

9 Church D, Brooks AJ. The effect of EFT (emotional freedom techniques) on psychological symptoms in addiction treatment: a pilot study. *International Journal of Scientific Research and Reports* 2013; 2.

10 Ranganathan VK, Siemionow V, Liu JZ, Sahgal V, Yue GH. From mental power to muscle power--gaining strength by using the mind. *Neuropsychologia* 2004; 42(7): 944-956.

Other sources

Church D, Wilde N. Emotional eating and weight loss following Skinny Genes, a six-week online program. Reported at the annual conference of the Association for Comprehensive Energy. *Psychology* (ACEP), Reston, VA. 2013.

De Bono E. *Mechanism of Mind* 1976. London, UK: Penguin Books ISBN-10: 0140137874.

Leach K. *Overweight Patient: A Psychological Approach to Understanding and Working with Obesity*. 2006. London, UK: Jessica Kingley.

Sojcher R, Perlman A, Fogerite S. Evidence and potential mechanisms for mindfulness practices and energy psychology for obesity and binge-eating disorder. *Explore: The Journal of Science and Healing* 2012; 8: 271-276. DOI:10.1016/j.explore.2012.06.003

Stapleton P, Sheldon T, Porter B. Clinical benefits of Emotional Freedom Techniques on food cravings at 12-months follow-up: a randomized controlled trial. *Energy Psychology: Theory, Research, and Treatment* 2012; 4: 1-12.

Stapleton P, Church D, Sheldon T, Porter B, Carlopio C. Depression symptoms improve after successful weight loss with EFT (Emotional Freedom Techniques): a randomized controlled trial. *Depression Research and Treatment*, In Press.

Stapleton P, Sheldon T, Porter B, Whitty J. A randomised clinical trial of a meridian-based intervention for food cravings with six-month follow-up. *Behaviour Change* 2011; 28: 1-16. DOI:10.1375/bech.28.1.1

Stapleton P, Sheldon T, Porter B. EFT Practitioner. Practical Application of Emotional Freedom Techniques for Food Cravings. *EFT Practitioner*. 2012. Wholistic Healing Publications.

Stapleton P, Sheldon T, Porter B. Clinical benefits of Emotional Freedom Techniques on food cravings at 12-months follow-up: a randomized controlled trial. *Energy Psychology: Theory, Research, & Treatment* 2012; 4(1): 13-24.

Online materials

Useful links

PSTEC www.pstec.org
The Success Clinic www.successclinic.com
Pat Carrington www.patcarrington.com
Lindsay Kenny www.lifecoachingwithlindsay.com
Rick Wilkes www.thrivingnow.com
Brad Yates www.bradyates.net

Resources

The following resources can be accessed from www.your7simplesteps.com

Pdf downloads

Worksheets

Your self-talk (page 56) *http://your7simplesteps.com/book1*
Limiting beliefs (page 58) *http://your7simplesteps.com/book2*
Timeline (page 62) *http://your7simplesteps.com/book3*
Resistance (page 64) *http://your7simplesteps.com/book4*
Dream-come-true (page 82) *http://your7simplesteps.com/book5*
Self-sabotage (page 85) *http://your7simplesteps.com/book6*
Accept yourself (page 92) *http://your7simplesteps.com/book7*
Comfort eating (page 108) *http://your7simplesteps.com/book8*
Secrets revealed (page 121) *http://your7simplesteps.com/book9*
Love and hate (page 129) *http://your7simplesteps.com/book10*
Fear of success (page 137) *http://your7simplesteps.com/book11*
Blocks to wellbeing (page 148) *http://your7simplesteps.com/book12*
Breaking through (page159) *http://your7simplesteps.com/book13*
Run-the-movie (page 161) *http://your7simplesteps.com/book14*

Remaining resistance (page 170) *http://your7simplesteps.com/book15*
Gratitude list (page 175) *http://your7simplesteps.com/book16*
Chart your success (page 178) *http://your7simplesteps.com/book17*

EFT aides memoire

EFT tapping template *http://your7simplesteps.com/book18*
EFT script template *http://your7simplesteps.com/book19*
9 Gamut point instructions *http://your7simplesteps.com/book20*
Seven Simple Steps check list *http://your7simplesteps.com/book21*
Food and mood diary template *http://your7simplesteps.com/book22*
Law of Attraction weight release chart *http://your7simplesteps.com/book23*

mp3 audio downloads

PSTEC free click tracks *http://your7simplesteps.com/book24*
Hypnosis to shrink your stomach *http://your7simplesteps.com/book25*
Hypnosis stress-buster *http://your7simplesteps.com/book26*
Hypnotic guided visualisation for a slimmer, healthier you *http://your7simplesteps.com/book27*

Video demonstrations of EFT

Increase your breathing EFT *http://your7simplesteps.com/book28*
Collapsing food cravings *http://your7simplesteps.com/book29*
Increasing metabolism *http://your7simplesteps.com/book30*

PSTEC materials

Free PSTEC click tracks *http://your7simplesteps.com/book31*
Listing and description of PSTEC optional tools *http://your7simplesteps.com/book32*

How to contact the authors

Sally Baker
Diploma Hypnotherapy
Advanced EFT Practitioner
Master Practitioner PSTEC
General Hypnotherapy Register (GHR)
Association of Meridian Therapies (AMT)
sally@workingonthebody.com
www.workingonthebody.com
London, England
Tel: +(44)7986 812 851
Skype: SallyEFT

Liz Hogon
Diploma Hypnotherapy (Adv)
Member International Association for Evidence-based Psychotherapy
(IAEBP)
Australian Hypnotherapists Association (MAHA)
Licensed Trainer Association of Meridian Therapists (AMT)
Master Practitioner PSTEC
liz@lizhogon.com
www.lizhogon.com
Melbourne, Australia
Tel: +(61)409 254 500
Skype: liz.hogon.hypnotherapy

Index

What our clients say about the techniques in this book

'In addition to weight loss, I am now more confident. I have forgotten any negative emotions from the past. I don't have anxieties anymore, and I feel in balance with myself.'

'I say that everyone needs some of this in their lives. I've tidied up my mind. I'm continuing with the plan. Weight loss is going at a slow rate, but it is happening, and I am not giving up!!! Very happy with everything.'

'I've had big emotional overeating issues for all of my 58 years and I was feeling resigned to becoming an unhealthy and overweight 60-year-old. Various changes in my life had made my problem seem quite insurmountable, but thanks to your help I have lost 18 pounds so far. I really feel now that next summer's big event will be the milestone birthday of a newly slim 60-year-old!'

'As a result of all the emotional churn up, I had the munchies at midnight. This time I tapped for a little while and what I actually ate was not that bad. I've noted it, forgiven myself, and am letting go. I am loosening food's hold over me, and it feels wonderful.'

'This worked for me after nothing else had for over 10 years. I released trapped emotions which kept me overeating; I recognised patterns and dealt with them. This works, and I am so grateful.'

'Have been around the block and back a few times with various therapies, but I had the most powerful healing ever with these processes.'

'I just don't believe it ... Yes, I do! ... No! I don't ... YES I DO !!! Three stone lost as of today!!! That is 42 pounds in 28 weeks!! Or 1.5 pounds per week! This is absolutely all down to this work – all supporting my round-the-mountain, round-the-park, round-the-shops walking, and my giving what I eat a higher priority than comforting feelings – especially the feelings of which I was not fully conscious.'

'I have felt a shift in myself already. I feel a sense of hope and anticipation, and I have successfully avoided eating anything chocolatey and sweet for a couple of weeks. Something seems to have clicked in for me. I have even been exercising a bit too – even I am surprised!'

'I'm thrilled as my bra size has reduced from 46 inches to 42 inches. Yesterday I bought myself some new leather gloves, and instead of buying a medium-to-large pair, the small-to-medium fitted me perfectly, and my shoe size has also changed from a seven to a six and a half – I'm even losing fat off my feet! I can do the zip up on my new size 22 trousers, and I plan that they will feel loose on me by the end of the month. But I have to say – best of all – I now wear size 22 knickers instead of size 32 and you know what? I haven't bought very many pairs of this new size, as I'm not finished yet, and more weight is still coming off!'

'Believe it or not, I AM really excited at the prospect of being a slim, "normal-sized" person who can go to any shop and buy clothes straight off the peg as well as looking, and feeling, healthier, more confident and happier.'

'Gave away my crisp (potato chips) stash from my office drawer – so no more carbs in that form anyway! One down and more to go!'

'I got on the scales this morning (my weekly ritual) and I have lost seven pounds! I am ecstatic and can't wait for my next session.'

'My mum certainly saw the difference in my face (i.e. slimmer!) but we both saw the difference when I put on the nightie I leave at her house. It was amazing to see the difference – it was no longer tight and you couldn't see my flesh through the material! I also got into the compact shower cubicle at her apartment with ease instead of struggling.'

'SUCCESS! I have just weighed myself and have lost another pound so I have now lost a whole stone (14 pounds) before going away on holiday!'

'There is definitely a spring in my step today – I lost three and a half pounds this week! I really feel I can reach my target weight loss of 28 pounds by the end of this month.'

'Went for blood tests last week and today got a clean bill of health in all areas – liver function, kidney function, very good level of sugar (i.e. low), low to regular level of cholesterol, so all good, and the doctor was very pleased to say the least.'

'I am now known in my office as "the incredible shrinking woman!"'

'What's the difference between heaven and hell? Well, hell is weighing food, counting calories, having to watch how much fruit I am eating and saying "no" to the things that I really like, such as cream and chocolate, and feeling like I am being "deprived". Heaven is being able to eat fruit, eat a bar of chocolate at the weekend, and feeling confident in choosing what I want to eat rather than just what is written on a diet plan. I have a real sense of freedom regarding my food choices, and it is spilling over to every area of my life. If this is what heaven is – give me more!'

'Here I am after three months and the weight is still coming off every week. But, the best part is that I am not dieting. For the first time in my life I'm not dieting but I'm losing weight. (Can you tell I still don't believe it?!!) I am so peaceful around food, and eating small portions – I even know how to listen to my body now when it tells me I'm full. That's never happened before.'

'It's all been so easy. No more struggle. No more staying home from parties because I had no control around food. I don't even notice the food there now as I'm too busy talking to people!'

'Feel like I have lots more energy, and I'm sleeping much better. (I don't understand how that works but I'm grateful!) I bought some new clothes on Saturday as the old ones are hanging off me now, and already I've dropped a dress size.'

'Three months on from my sessions and I have lost two stones [28 pounds/13 kilograms] which is great but the best part is that this has helped me change how I view and eat my food to the point that I not only believe I will achieve my goal but I will also maintain it. I love food, always have and always will – the difference now is that I do eat everything I enjoy but in moderation – my eating speed has slowed down tremendously, which means I end up eating a lot less because I realise I'm full.'

'Got some good news yesterday – my regular three-month blood test shows a big drop in blood glucose and, with drugs and diet, I'm in the non-diabetic normal range!!!!!!! Well done me!!!!!!!! My cholesterol has improved a lot too!!'

'The main difficulty I have is even remembering what the issues were that I did PSTEC on. It collapsed them so completely that it is as if they never existed – that's how well they've worked for me!'

'After the session I needed some space to carrying on processing. I gave my imagination free rein (risky!) and I visualised unravelling the fat from my tummy like unravelling wool from an old jumper – something I used to do a lot as a child (the wool not the fat!). I also imagined that each time I have a pee I'm peeing out droplets of fat. I feel that I'm releasing the fat. In fact I'm reminding myself to give my body permission to release the fat it's held onto all this time.'

'My blood glucose levels are continuing to drop. This morning I had another new morning fasting level of 5.7, so that's three times this week. Yesterday I had my lowest ever reading of 4.8 and I didn't feel crap. My body is adjusting to the lower levels. I'm getting used to the idea, and liking it, that change is not only possible, but it's happening!!!'

'For far too long I have felt weighed down and held back by a number of painful emotional "boulders"! With this incredible help I have found ways to either let go of the ongoing physical, and emotional pain completely, or to find a way of "living with" the experiences so that they no longer hurt or damage me. I no longer feel scared and depressed. I'm feeling happier and physically and emotionally "lighter". I'm in my 50s and I've now been freed to be more fully myself out in the world, and to stop hiding my light!'

'Physically I'm really aware of my abdomen and the whole of me knows that something big has shifted. Knowing where my feelings of anxiety stem from has helped me to understand better why it has always been so important for me to know what's going on around me with the children, with BH, and at work. Deep down I'm scared, and when I'm aware stuff is happening I need to know exactly what it is as it triggers all my old anxieties. Hence my controlling, and interfering behaviour, and why it's with my family and not in my work-place. These incredible insights mean I feel ready to change that behaviour as I'm now longer afraid.'

'It's a cliché, of course – all those years learning how to help other people have brought me to the place to finally be able to help myself. To give to me what I've given to others. At the point that I embrace and accept my ability to help others I now believe and trust that it can have the same healing effect on me. Yesterday I fully felt and experienced me caring for the scared little child inside of me. And I'm still feeling it...'